JOHN ABBOTT

John Abbott appeared in over eighty stage productions during his career as an actor, and became a member of the Royal Shakespeare Company. He played Alonso in Mark Rylance's production of *The Tempest* and was Master of Sonnets at Shakespeare's Globe. He made many appearances on television, including *Doctor Who*, *Bottom*, *Poirot* and *The Vicar of Dibley*. He also appeared in *Four Weddings and a Funeral* with Hugh Grant and *Treasure Island* with Charlton Heston and Christian Bale.

John became an acting teacher in adult education and then moved on to further education, teaching at City and Islington College, and Chelsea and Westminster College. He obtained a Master's degree in Performance at Middlesex University, where he was then invited to teach on the BA in Acting course.

When Jane Harrison became Head of Acting at Mountview she asked him to teach improvisation and direct projects on the BA, and when she moved to ArtsEd she brought him with her as a full-time member of the teaching staff. He became Head of Academic Studies and wrote the course document with Jane Harrison that enabled the course to become validated as a BA in Acting by City University.

As a teacher at ArtsEd, John refined his improvisation course, focusing on its use as a creative tool for actors. He also taught stand-up, Shakespeare and audition/interview technique. He directed many second-year plays, including *Hamlet*, *A View from the Bridge*, *Arturo Ui*, *A Midsummer Night's Dream* and *A Streetcar Named Desire*. John eventually became Head of the Acting course where he stayed until his retirement in 2012.

His other books – *The Improvisation Book*, *Improvisation in Rehearsal* and *The Acting Book* – are all published by Nick Hern Books.

LEO WOODALL

Leo Woodall graduated from Arts Educational School (ArtsEd) with a BA in Acting, and has since gone on to appear in *The White Lotus* (HBO), *One Day* (Netflix), *Citadel* (Amazon Prime) and *Prime Target* (Apple TV+).

THE DRAMA SCHOOL HANDBOOK

Getting In, Getting On and Getting Out There

John Abbott

NHB

NICK HERN BOOKS
London
www.nickhernbooks.co.uk

A Nick Hern Book

The Actor Training Handbook
first published in Great Britain in 2024
by Nick Hern Books Limited,
The Glasshouse, 49a Goldhawk Road,
London W12 8QP

Copyright © 2024 John Abbott
Foreword copyright © 2024 Leo Woodall

John Abbott has asserted his moral right
to be identified as the author of this work

Designed and typeset by Nick Hern Books
Printed and bound in Great Britain by Halstan Ltd

A CIP catalogue record for this book is available
from the British Library

ISBN 978 1 84842 690 0

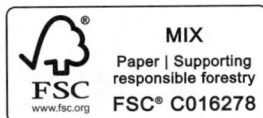

MIX
Paper | Supporting
responsible forestry
FSC
www.fsc.org
FSC® C016278

For Jane Harrison

CONTENTS

FOREWORD

Leo Woodall

When I was thinking about auditioning for drama school I had very little experience and very little confidence. I needed help. Which speeches to choose, how to perform them truthfully under pressure, even how to walk into the room.

I needed John Abbott.

I can honestly say that without his guidance I would never have auditioned with the confidence needed to get into one of the leading UK drama schools. It was brilliant, and I truly believe I wouldn't have been accepted without him!

Once I was a drama student I panicked because everyone seemed so good, they knew what they were doing and what they were talking about. Surely the teachers would realise they had made a mistake and ask me to leave. I even walked into the Head of Acting's office with the Principal of the school and told them I didn't think I should be there.

I needed John Abbott.

Once again he talked me through the ups and downs of training and got me on the right track. We would meet regularly to discuss how it was going and with his guidance I was able to navigate the excitement of great casting; the disappointment of not-such-great casting; different styles of teaching; relationships with other students; and much, much more.

He also gave me exceptional advice for actually moving into the career I so wanted. How to talk to agents with confidence, how to make self-tapes, and how to join the profession as an equal.

Now I've graduated and I travel the world filming, taking direction, meeting new people – and John's words come back to me time and time again, and now he has put all the help he gave me into this book.

Trust me: you will also need John Abbott!

ACKNOWLEDGEMENTS

First, I've got to thank **Jane Morton**. This book wouldn't exist if she hadn't asked me to help her son Leo with his audition speeches to get in to drama school.

Then, of course, thanks to **Leo Woodall** himself, who was with me through the whole process. Together we worked on all the things that drama schools are actually looking for in prospective students. Then, once he was at drama school, we met regularly to discuss some of the problems facing students that might not get noticed by the staff.

Also thanks to **Laura Meredith**, who gave me an insight into the student experience from a female prospective.

I must also thank **Gareth Farr** for the many conversations we had about how teachers and students interact with each other.

And **Leanne Nagle**, who gave me some good advice for the third section of the book on how to use technology and social media.

I also have to thank **Yusuf Kahmisa**, who arranged an extended meeting with a group of foundation course students to help me understand the mindset of prospective drama school students.

And thanks to **Paul Martin** at **Sainou Talent Agency** for keeping me up to date on how actors use the internet for interviews and auditions.

Then thanks to **everyone** at **Nick Hern Books** for their publishing talents and hard work:

Matt Applewhite, who has been a friend and colleague for nearly twenty years and seen me through four books.

Sarah Lambie, who was an enthusiastic, patient and supportive editor of this book.

Deborah Halsey, who made the pages look great.

And, of course, **Nick Hern** himself, without whom...

PART ONE

GETTING IN

1. FIRST STEPS

So let's start from the moment you decide to get some actor training.

What do you do next?

Well... maybe you're at secondary school and a **famous Hollywood producer** is scouring England looking for an **untrained teenager** to star in his next movie and he picks you out.

You end up going to Hollywood and becoming an international superstar.

Yes indeed!

Or perhaps your English teacher has a friend who is **a casting director for the Royal Shakespeare Company.**

He recommends you for the part of Romeo...

And you wow all the critics!!

Or maybe you're in a show at your further education college, and **a top actors' agent sees you and...**

Stop!

Stop!

Stop!

Stop dreaming!

A very fine actress I met once said the difference between amateur actors and professional actors is that professional actors '**dedicate their lives to acting**'.

Think about that before you head out on this journey.

They dedicate their lives to acting.

Is that what you want?

If it is, carry on reading.

GETTING ADVICE

Okay, so perhaps you need some advice on how to get started.

But listen. **Don't ask an actor, whatever you do!** They can be a bit cynical.

After all, if someone has **dedicated their life to acting** and they haven't got a job, it can make them feel quite depressed.

Actors often get depressed.

But don't worry, people in **all manner of jobs** get depressed at one time or another.

In fact, statistics show that the job that makes you most depressed is being a dentist!

So don't be a dentist, right?

MIGHT AS WELL BE AN ACTOR.

Hey! Perhaps your **drama teacher** will be able to give you advice.

Or maybe you could try a **Google search**.

How about standing outside a **West End stage door** after a show and stopping a **famous actress** as she emerges to ask her **how she started**? You never know. **You might strike lucky.**

All these things are possible.

But probably the best thing to do if you want to be an actor is to apply for a place in **a recognised drama school**, so you **can get some training**. If you do that:

○ You will meet other people **your own age** who want to be actors.
○ You'll learn loads of **techniques** from experts.
○ You'll be in lots of **plays.**
○ And you'll get an introduction to the world of **professional acting**.

Sounds good?

Then do it!

FINDING A DRAMA SCHOOL

When to apply

Most drama schools start their audition process during the **Autumn Term** and then continue with regular audition days until **the middle of the Summer Term**.

So you should begin the process **well over a year before you want to do your training**.

Most drama schools need applications to be in by February or March for the following September.

How to choose

All the drama schools have websites explaining **how brilliant they are**, and they will all have pictures of **ex-students who have been successful** so it's a minefield.

But this is where your **dedication to your ambition** starts.

Get online to check out drama schools.

Read their websites carefully.

And get a *gut feeling* of which schools appeal to you!

They all **teach acting** but they each have their own **method**, so it's important to think about what **you actually want to learn**.

And what kind of career you would like to have.

- ○ Maybe you want to be in a **long-running television drama**.
- ○ Or maybe you want to make your mark in a **TV sitcom**.
- ○ Perhaps you want to be part of an **experimental theatre group**.

- ○ Or make cutting-edge, **new-wave films**.
- ○ Maybe you want to perform at **the National Theatre**.
- ○ Or maybe you want to be a **movie star**.

There are many paths available so **you should think carefully about what you actually want**.

You probably like watching **films** and **TV**.

Maybe you like going to the **theatre**.

And there are probably **actors you particularly admire**.

So find out where they were trained.

Especially if they have recently graduated.

You should also:

- ○ Check out the drama schools' **specialist facilities**, such as rehearsal studios, theatres, and radio, film and television studios.
- ○ Find out about **tutor contact time**.
- ○ Discover the **length of a normal training day**.
- ○ Find the names of the **professional directors** they use – Google them to see how connected they are to the industry.

Checking out the schools you've chosen

If it's at all possible, **try to see some final-year productions at your selected drama schools** so you can judge the kind of work they are doing.

- ○ Are the plays mainly **classical** or are they **contemporary**?
- ○ Is the acting style theatrical, humorous, physical or an example of ultra-realism? **Ask yourself which styles you are most interested in.**
- ○ Do the students look **confident on stage**?
- ○ Hang around after the performance to **observe the atmosphere** when the cast emerge from their dressing rooms.
- ○ Watch how **members of staff talk to the students** after the performance to see if they have the sort of relationship that would like to have with your teachers.

Ask yourself if you would have liked to have been in the show!

This is your training.

And you need it to be the best.

So you can achieve your ambition.

Making your application

Drama schools **charge you a fee to audition** so, unless you're very rich, you will have to be quite selective.

I suggest you apply to about six drama schools if you can afford it.

Sometimes you will be asked to fill in an application form **online**, so that will be easy.

○ Write about your **acting experience**.

○ Write about your **other interests**.

○ Be enthusiastic **but don't exaggerate**.

○ Be **straightforward** and **honest** about yourself.

○ Tell them what you want to **achieve** and how you think **they can help**.

THE AUDITION PROCESS

This is different for each drama school, but they all want to know

✓ Can you **act**?

✓ What **experience have you had** of acting?

✓ **What are you like** as a person?

Most drama schools ask to see a self-tape to start with.

Check online for details of what each drama school wants you to do.

And how they want you to do it.

(*And turn to page 186 in Chapter Thirteen for advice on self-tapes.*)

After they have viewed your self-tape they will then decide **if their training is suitable for you**. If they think it is, you will then be given **an audition date** for some time in the future!

That's exciting!

(*Note: Choosing audition speeches and preparing them for performance is the same for self-tapes as it is for live auditions.*)

Gathering suitable audition speeches

Drama schools usually ask to see you doing two speeches:

> **A classical speech** – some ask specifically for a **speech from a Shakespeare play.**
>
> And **a contemporary speech** – which some drama schools call a **modern speech.**

Maybe they will ask you to **prepare a song** as well.

> And perhaps you need an **extra speech** up your sleeve.
>
> And you may have to do a bit of **sight-reading**.

Each drama school has its own **particular requirements**. But basically, the standby reliable requirements are the two speeches:

A classical speech and a contemporary speech.

The classical speech

A classical speech is one that uses **heightened language** and often contains **metaphors, similes and poetic images.**

In other words it is not entirely naturalistic.

And was probably written over four hundred years ago!

In those days the **words the actors spoke** had to let the audience know about:

○ Their character's **mood and inner feelings.**

○ Where their character **is supposed to be.**

- What **time of day** it is.
- And probably **what the weather was like**!

The audience went to the theatre to *hear* a play.

- There was **no stage lighting** because the performances always took place in daylight.
- There were **no recorded sound effects**.
- There were **no sets** to speak of.
- And usually there were **no elaborate costumes**.

Everything the audience needed to know, they got from the words the actors spoke.

Look at these lines from Shakespeare's *King Lear*:

> LEAR *Blow, winds, and crack your cheeks! Rage! Blow!*
> *You cataracts and hurricanoes, spout*
> *Till you have drench'd our steeples, drown'd the cocks!*
> *You sulphurous and thought-executing fires,*
> *Vaunt-couriers to oak-cleaving thunderbolts*
> *Singe my white head! And thou, all-shaking thunder,*
> *Strike flat the thick rotundity o' the world!*

The weather, right?

I told you so!

Even if you don't understand every word, it's pretty clear that Lear is **in the middle of the most horrendous thunderstorm**.

So that is why I say that a classical speech uses heightened language and **is not entirely naturalistic**.

Of course it has to be acted realistically.

But it also gives the audience loads of information.

And it's poetry!

Tricky stuff for sure.

But fun too!!

The safe bet for a classical speech is to do one from a **Shakespeare** play.

○ Although it would be quite acceptable to do something from another Elizabethan or Jacobean playwright, like **Marlowe**, **Webster** or **Fletcher**.

○ You could even do a speech from one of the **Ancient Greek playwrights** like **Aeschylus**, **Euripides** or **Sophocles**. These are all perfectly acceptable, although trawling through these **difficult texts** for an appropriate speech can be quite a mission.

○ **Warning!** You might think that **Restoration comedy** is classical. Or **Chekhov**. Or **Ibsen**, **Oscar Wilde** or **Noël Coward**. But most drama schools wouldn't consider them to be officially 'classical'.

So it would be best to avoid them.

Why annoy anyone before you've even started?

Which classical speech?

Okay. Let me lay my cards on the table here:

If you choose a speech from a Shakespeare play, it is impossible to find one that no one else will be doing.

People holding auditions often hear the same Shakespeare speeches, **because they are the ones that are good for young actors**.

'I left no ring with her. What means this lady?' (Viola from *Twelfth Night*)

Or

'Think not I love him, though I ask for him.' (Phoebe from *As You Like It*)

But the popularity of these speeches never clouds the panel's judgement of the acting talent on display.

So originality in the choice of a classical speech is **not a major requirement**.

Don't get hung up on it.

It's much more important to choose a speech that is **suitable for your personality and age**. So don't go for *King Lear*. He's ancient.

I suggest that you choose a character who is **no more than fifteen years older than yourself**.

There are **books of classical audition speeches** and it is worth looking through those, but don't reject speeches just because you don't understand them on first reading.

Shakespeare is hard for everyone to understand.

So take it slowly.

And read the speeches carefully before making your choices.

The contemporary speech

There are also **books of contemporary speeches** that you can look through.

But maybe you had a speech in a play **at college** or **in a drama group** that you liked.

And maybe it went down well!

If that's the case, then it would be a good idea to do it for your audition speech.

○ For a start, you will already have **done a lot of work** on it.
○ And secondly, you will **know the play it came from backwards**.

People are sometimes so obsessed with finding something 'new' that they dismiss their past successes.

Of course you may not have had the **opportunity** of doing a speech like that.

But never mind.

That's not a problem.

It just means a bit more work.

Here's some other suggestions:

- ○ Keep your eyes and ears open for speeches **when you go to see plays.**
- ○ The theatre might even be **selling the playtext at a special reduced price,** so you can buy it to read later.
- ○ Visit **the National Theatre Bookshop.** They have a great selection of plays and theatre books.
- ○ Otherwise, **go to a local library or a bookshop** and just keep searching through the play section until something catches your eye.
- ○ If you live outside London, find out if there is a **theatre near you** that has a bookshop or library.

But, please,

An important piece of advice...

Don't try to shock the audition panel by your choice of outrageous material!

For a start, **an audition panel is unshockable.** They've seen it all.

- ○ I've heard speeches with **way too much swearing.**
- ○ I've seen **simulated masturbation.**
- ○ I've sat though **blood-curdling mutilation** speeches.
- ○ I've heard descriptions of **deviant sexual practices.**
- ○ I've even had a girl **baring her breasts** in an audition.

None of these things have ever shocked me.

Or made me feel that the actor is amazingly brave.

Or even interesting.

I just get **embarrassed** because it makes them seem *so desperate*.

So please don't try to show how shocking you can be.

People just want to see if you can act!

The length of an audition speech

It's frightening to hear this, but **the audition panel usually make up their mind**

Within 30 seconds of you starting your speech!

It's true.

1. They may have decided to **reject you after 30 seconds**, in which case you might as well **get it over with as quickly as possible.**

Or... wait for it...

2. **They may recognise your talent immediately!** And a long speech could possibly **make them change their mind!**

Oops !!

So unless the drama school says differently, your audition speeches should last just over a minute and a half each.

And definitely no longer than two minutes.

That's all the time you need.

And remember this:

> ### The worst thing you can do is to bore the audition panel.

Character choices

The type of character you play doesn't need to be extreme to be effective.

In fact, it is quite a good idea to use speeches in which the characters have the same sort of emotions **that you have experienced yourself.**

O   Most people know what it's like **to fall in love**, so either **Romeo** or **Juliet** would probably be characters you could choose.

- Maybe you sometimes **get angry**, so a speech where your character loses their temper would be useful.
- Perhaps you find it easy to **make people laugh**, so try a funny speech.
- Or if you like **explaining things**, choose a speech in which your character tells someone about something.

Find speeches that you really relate to!

Contrasting speeches

Once you have selected one of your speeches, make sure the other has a different mood or emotion.

a) A **strong, confident character** for your classical, for instance.

b) And an **uncertain, romantic character** for the contemporary.

I bet you've experienced **both these moods** at one time or another.

a) Maybe a **loud, bombastic** speech for one.

b) And a **quiet, intense** speech for the other.

The contrasting moods in the speeches should both be moods and emotions **you experience yourself**.

Sometimes you are *happy*, sometimes you are *sad*.

Sometimes you feel *full of energy*, sometimes you feel *knackered*.

These are the sorts of contrasts you should be looking for.

CONCLUSION

When you're preparing for a drama school audition, it's no good thinking 'that will do', about any step on the path.

Nothing will ever just 'do'.

It can always be improved.

○ If you feel **confident with your speech** make sure that **you can still do it when you're nervous.**

○ If you are in a **bad mood** on the day of the audition, you must be **positive when you do your speeches.**

○ If you are **tired, depressed** or you still need to be able to perform **an upbeat, lively speech.**

It's no good coming out of an audition and blaming yourself for **not being in the right mood.**

You have to make sure that you are *always* in the right mood.

You have to be at your best *whatever the circumstances.*

And that means lots and lots of work.

Just remember...

You don't *have* to be an actor.

It's just a choice!

But if you make that choice,

You need to do everything you can to beat the competition!

I mean it...

EVERYTHING!

2. PREPARING YOUR SPEECHES

So now it's time to start getting serious.

You want this, right?

Well... the next thing to understand is:

How to impress the audition panel.

And actually that's quite easy because they are only interested in two things:

COMMITMENT & TALENT

I'll deal with **talent** in the next chapter, but this chapter is about how to show the audition panel that you are **committed to your work**.

Let's start with an important reality check.

Doing an audition speech has nothing to do with *real acting*.

Shock-horror, shock-horror!

And why not?

As a professional actor you are trying to ***hide* your acting skills from the audience** so they believe your character is a real person.

When you are doing an audition speech you are trying **to *reveal* your acting skills to the audition panel** so they will want to offer you a place on their acting course.

That's the difference!

And actually there's another difference.

In plays and films the characters are usually **talking to each other**. The trouble with an audition speech is that **there is no one there to actually talk to**.

You are on your own.

'Ah,' you may say, 'but this speech is a **monologue from a play** and the actor was on their own when they said it.'

Oh no they weren't!

There was an audience out there.

And the actor was communicating with them.

'But isn't the **audition panel** an audience?'

No... it's not!

It's a collection of judgemental observers!

Who might even be taking notes!

HELP ‼

So this chapter and the next are about how you can **prepare your audition speech** in such a way that it will show **'a collection of judgemental observers'** that you have **the COMMITMENT and TALENT to become a professional actor**.

BECOMING FAMILIAR WITH THE PLAY

Let's start from the moment you have chosen your audition speeches.

What do you do next?

Read the plays

It's no good just knowing the words of your speeches, you have to **find out as much as you can** about your **characters** and the **situations they're in**.

Most of that information will be in the text of the play.

(*Note: Obviously a **Shakespeare** play is difficult to read, but you can find editions of his popular plays with a modern-language translation running alongside the original text. Some people say that this is cheating and you should struggle with Shakespeare's own words, but* *you're not applying for a degree in English Literature! You just want to find out what the play's about so you can make sense of the speech. So give yourself a break!)*

Here's where your **commitment** begins.

Read the play so you have some idea of the story.

And then...

Read it again!

And make some notes about your character as you do it.

One of the most useful things you can do is to:

○ Write a list of **everything that your character says about themselves**.

○ And then write another list of **everything that other people in the play say about your character**.

○ **Then you can compare the two lists.**

This way you will be able to **make your *own* decisions** about the character.

After you've made your lists you should **read the play yet again** so you become as familiar with it as you would be if you were performing **the whole thing**. There are two reasons for this:

1. It will help you learn **as much about your character as possible**.

2. You will be able to **answer any questions about the play** that the audition panel might ask you after you've done your speech.

This second reason is really important.

It will show the panel that you are committed to the work.

But there's something else:

If you can't answer their questions you will feel useless!

And your confidence will crumble!

And *staying confident* is one of the most important things on the day of the audition!

Research

Sometimes the play takes place **in a part of the world that you are unfamiliar with**.

Sometimes there are **things about the character** that are **outside your field of experience.**

If either of these things are the case, you should **start doing some research.**

Luckily research is easy because we have **the internet.**

○ **Google everything** and take notes.
○ **Think about** what you are reading.
○ **Decide** how it will impact on your character.

**The more you know about the background
of a character, the better prepared you will be
to play the part.**

Copying the way other actors perform your speeches

This is a total no-no!

It doesn't matter how brilliantly another actor does a speech or how much you admire them, **you should *never* try to copy someone else's performance.**

There is only one way of interpreting a part

And that is your way!

Never forget:

The brilliant actor you admire **only had the same information as you** when they started work.

So read the play thoroughly and do some research.

**Then you will have all the information you need
to create your own unique version of the speech.**

Think like your character thinks

Imagination is the actor's greatest tool so now is the time to use it so you can create a **well-rounded character.**

Here's what to do:

Imagine you are your character.

Then write answers to the following twenty-four questions **the way your character would.**

Some of the questions will be easy to answer, but the others will need a bit of thought.

○ So **think** like your character.

○ Use your **instincts.**

○ And just **make things up**!

Remember:

If you have studied the play properly

And done your research,

There are no wrong answers.

Character questions

1. What is your full name?

2. Do you have a nickname or pet name?

3. What is your relationship with other members of your family?

4. What is your greatest responsibility?

5. Do you have a social life?

6. What sort of people do you like to be with?

7. What is your job?

8. What is your state of health?

9. What is the state of your mental health?

10. What kind of education did you have?

11. What makes you laugh?

12. What makes you cry?

13. What moves you emotionally?

14. How sexual/sensual are you?

15. How interested are you in your appearance?

16. What do you daydream about?

17. What would catch your attention or distract you?

18. Are you relaxed, hyper or something in between?

19. What is your ambition?

20. Do you like yourself?

21. Do you like other people?

22. What are you obsessed about?

23. Are you a good listener?

24. Do you like Art or Science?

(*Note: When you do this you should indicate the question in the way you write the answer so you can read through them later without having to look at the questions. e.g. 1. My name is Mary Smith; 2. My nickname is Curly; and so on.*)

Pretending to be your character

You've done lots of research.

You've done lots of thinking.

Now you are ready to start acting.

Hurrah!!

Using the knowledge you have gained so far, spend a bit of time going through **the following list of activities.**

Explore each one until you have learned something.

(*Note: This doesn't involve any speaking. Just use your imagination and see what happens.*)

○ Walk around the room **pretending to be your character.**
○ Think about the things **your character would think** about as you walk.
○ Try sitting in a chair to see **how your character would sit down.**
○ Try **standing up**...

- **Lying down on the floor...**
- **Looking out of the window.** What would your character see and **how would they feel about it?**
- Try feeling like your character **as much as you can.**
- Walk out of the room and then walk back in the room as if your character was **seeing it for the first time.**
- **Examine the room.**
- Try **going for a walk outside** pretending to be your character. Walk in the **park.** Walk down a **busy shopping street.** See things **the way your character would see them** and think about your character's opinion of everything.
- **Try to get inside the head of your character.**

> **Pretending to be someone else is the main foundation of acting on which everything else rests.**

Learning your lines

Learning lines can be the most boring part of being an actor because it's basically **hard work** and **repetition.**

But here are a couple of suggestions:

- As you learn the words, try to get a **sequence of thoughts** going through the speech so **each thought leads to the next.**
- Try learning your lines **late at night.** For some reason they stay in your brain better.
- When you think you know your lines roughly, think through the words **just before you go to sleep.** If you get stuck, **keep thinking until you remember the next line.** If that doesn't work, look at the text and then force yourself to make a link from one line to the next.
- It will be easier to learn a classical speech if you work out **exactly what it all means** before you start memorising.

Learn your lines thoroughly. You may think you know your lines pretty well, but the pressure of doing the speech **in front of an audition panel** can easily make you forget them.

Learn your lines accurately. The audition panel will have heard many of the speeches before and they will know **if you haven't learned the lines accurately.**

And they might think you haven't prepared properly.

Ouch !!

Zero points for commitment!

You need to know the words so well that you can race through them.

Even when you're doing the washing-up.

I mean it.

(Note: Classical texts have to be learned absolutely correctly. Word for word. No excuses.)

Showing the speeches to other people

There is a terrible temptation to ask friends and family what they think, **but don't show them your speeches just yet.**

They are too close to you.

○ They don't know what drama schools **are looking for.**

○ They are not used to seeing **work in progress.**

○ They can't get their heads around **seeing you being someone else.**

So practise on your own.

Trust your instincts.

And let your gut feelings guide you!

WARM-UPS

Before you start practising your speeches you need to **clear your mind of all other thoughts** so you are **physically and mentally ready to work.**

I suggest you use the following routine **each time** you have a practice session.

1. Physical warm-up

○ Try **jumping up and down** and **running around a bit** if you've got space.

○ **Stand on one leg and shake the other.** Then reverse it.

○ **Lift your shoulders, roll them around a bit and then let them drop.** Do this several times.

○ **Shake each arm** from the shoulders right the way down to your hands.

○ Stand with your feet apart and **roll your hips around**.

○ **Stretch out your fingers** and then **shake them loose.**

○ Put on some **dance music** and try to express the rhythm and melody you hear **by moving different parts of your body**.

Be bold with all of this.

No one's watching!

2. Vocal warm-up

○ Try **chewing with your whole face** so all the muscles are moving.

○ **Blow through your lips** so they vibrate against each other as if you are cold.

○ See how wide you can **stretch your eyes and mouth** and then **scrunch them up as tight as you can**. Do this several times.

○ **Stretch your tongue out** and **move it from side to side**.

○ **Keep repeating 'Lah, lah, lah... lee, lee, lee... lay, lay, lay...'** to get your tongue moving.

○ And then **repeat 'Bah, bah, bah... bow, bow, bow... boo, boo, boo...'** for your lips.

○ **Say a long deep and satisfied, 'Ahh...'** and feel the sound vibrating around your chest and throat.

Do these simple exercises for a few minutes to get yourself vocally ready.

3. Mental warm-up

While you are doing these exercises try to **empty your brain** of any day-to-day problems you might have.

○ Then sit in a chair and **shut your eyes**.

○ Don't think about the speech just yet.

○ Think of yourself as **an actor**.

○ Focus on **what you are about to do.**

○ Finally, start thinking about **the character you are about to become.**

4. Speech warm-up

○ Stand up and run around or jump up and down, saying the words of your speech as fast as you can.

(*Note: You should try to make sense of the speech as you do this but the most important thing is to **make sure you really know the words**. It's no good if you are still trying to remember them while you are **doing your audition**; they have to be in there, **ready to flow out** whenever you need them. **Like real life.**)*

5. *Messing around with the speech*

For the last part of your warm-up routine you should try messing around with your speech **so it becomes like an old friend.**

Here are a few ways to loosen it up. Try a couple of them each practice session...

And have fun doing it.

Do the speech:

○ as a scene from **a rubbish television series.**

○ as a romantic **Disney** character.

○ as a scene from a **scary horror film.**

○ as an aria from an **opera** (sing it).

○ as a scene from a **pantomime.**

○ as a **reality-TV show** like *Big Brother* or *I'm a Celebrity.*

○ as a scene from a **silent film** (no words).

○ as a scene from a **West End musical.**

○ as a scene from a **slap-stick comedy.**

○ as a **political speech** in Parliament.

○ as a piece of **physical theatre.**

○ as a scene from a **popular kids' cartoon.**

(*Note: Never rehearse your audition speech without first doing all your warm-ups. Then you will be ready to work.*)

TRANSFORMATION

Transformation for **auditions** isn't about wigs, costumes and make-up.

It's about the way your characters *think*.

How they *move*.

And how they *express themselves*.

Emotional transformation

When you're working on an **emotional transformation** you should think about **your own emotional experiences**:

○ If your character is a **lover**, behave as you do **when you are in love**.

○ If your character is **nervous**, use **your own nervousness**.

○ If your character seems **happy**, behave the way you do when **you are happy**.

○ If **frightened**, let them be like you are **when you are frightened**.

The person you know most about is yourself.

Use that knowledge to create truthful emotional transformations.

Physical transformation

When you are working on a **physical transformation** you should think about the different things that might affect how your character moves:

○ The amount of **energy** your character has.

○ The way your character **feels about themself** – confident, nervous, shy, dreamy, etc.

○ Your character's **state of health.**

○ What your character **does** on a daily basis.

Find the physicality within yourself.

Never go for stereotypes.

If your character is a **princess, a soldier, a factory worker** or a **film star**, just behave how *you* **would behave if** *you* **were any of these.**

Characters are **people just like you** and in different circumstances you could have ended up as a **princess, a soldier, a factory worker** or a **film star.**

So think about the life your character leads.

And then find the physicality *you* **would have if** *you* **led that life.**

Do that and you will always be creating a unique and truthful physicality.

VARYING THE SPEECH

When you are acting in a play or film you are doing **several things at the same time**:

1. You are trying to make the character **truthful for yourself.**

2. You are trying to **communicate your character's thoughts and words** to the other characters.

3. You are trying to **listen and respond** to other characters.

4. You are trying to **tell a story to the audience.** (*Never forget this.*)

5. You are trying to **entertain the audience.** (*Don't forget this either.*)

So when you know the words thoroughly it's a good idea to **explore each of these things in isolation.**

(*Note: The following exercises are simply to help you add subtlety and nuance to your speeches. None of them will be the way you actually perform them in the audition. That will come later.*)

Finding the truth for yourself

○ Ignore what your character is supposed to be doing and **sit quietly in a chair.**

○ Then start **whispering the words of the speech to yourself** as if you are trying to think through your character's inner thoughts.

Communicating the words

○ Imagine you are in the middle of an empty field and **shout the words as clearly and as carefully as you can**. Imagine you are trying to communicate with the gods. (*Try this outside so you don't disturb the neighbours.*)

Communicating the thoughts

○ Say the speech to your pet and try to **make it understand what you're talking about**. (*If you haven't got a pet, a soft toy, a plastic superhero, or even a houseplant will do.*)

Communicating with clarity

○ Sit in a chair and imagine you are surrounded by a group of five-year-olds who are sitting cross-legged on the floor in front of you. **Say the speech carefully using the inflections you would use to a five-year-old** to help them understand what you are saying.

Creating imaginary reactions

(*This next exercise breaks the speech down and will take ages to do, but don't worry. It's just an exploration.*)

○ Place two chairs facing each other so you can sit in one of them and **imagine you are talking to someone** sitting in the other.

○ Say each phrase or sentence with **the strong mental attitude of 'Do you understand what I'm saying?'**

○ Pause at the end of each phrase or sentence and **imagine that the other person is saying 'Yes I understand.'**

○ Don't continue with the next phrase or sentence **until you are sure the imaginary person has really understood**.

(*Note: Later on, when you are ready to show your speech to a friend or a drama teacher, you can try this exercise with a real person. Ask them to think about what you are saying and respond with the words 'Yes I understand' after each phrase or sentence.*)

Keeping the listener interested

○ Say the speech as if you are **a stand-up comedian** in front of an audience. Be bold and clear as you do it. (*There is no need to be funny. Just make sure **you keep the audience interested.***)

○ Say the speech as if you are **a magician** trying to **surprise the audience** or **make them jump**.

○ Say the speech like **a storyteller** trying to **thrill the audience.** Have them **on the edge of their seats**.

○ See if you can **make the audience love you** when you say the speech.

○ Then see if you can **make them hate you**.

○ **Put all these ideas together** and **see how entertaining and varied** you can be with your speech.

(*Note: As I said, none of these exercises will be the way you actually perform the speech in the audition, they are just to help you find variety and give you new ideas.*)

A FEW TECHNICAL SUGGESTIONS

Putting an imaginary character into the scene

When your character is talking to an imaginary person you must make sure **you know exactly who you are talking to**.

○ Imagine you are talking to **someone you know** so you will be familiar with **how they would react**.

○ Place your imaginary person **downstage and slightly to the left or right of centre** so you are more or less facing the front.

The audition panel needs to see your face.

(*Note: There are always exceptions to this rule. For instance, you might be doing a speech in which **your character is sitting on a park bench with the other character**. In that case you can use two chairs to create a park bench, but **always perform the speech so you are facing the audition panel as much as possible**.*)

○ Make sure the imaginary listener really **understands everything you say.**

Communication is a vital part of acting.

Speaking your thoughts out loud

In **classical monologues** the characters are often **speaking their inner thoughts out loud**.

○ Sometimes they are **thinking through a set of problems**.

○ Or **debating with themselves**.

○ Perhaps they are **making plans for the future**.

○ Or they could be **telling the audience how they are feeling**.

○ Or maybe they are simply **entertaining themselves with their ideas**.

Ask yourself **why your character is speaking out loud** when there is no one around to listen to them.

It's important for you to know that.

(*Note: Classical characters sometimes tell lies when they are talking to other characters in the play, but when they have a monologue they are usually speaking the truth about themselves. Also, some of these classical characters can be quite evil but it would be wrong to think that they are insane.*)

Making the speech come alive

Some people like to work out exactly how to say each line of a speech so they can repeat it perfectly every time.

But this can be **dangerous**.

It can make the speech seem *lifeless* and *dull!*

Oh no!

So I'm going to recommend a different approach.

If you want to **bring life to a speech** it's best to make **yourself feel alive** as you perform it.

Whenever you are practising your speech, always be **open to new ways of saying a line, or thinking a thought**.

Even when you're in the middle of the speech.

You may have thought of a particularly good way of saying a line yesterday, but *today* it's more important to feel **the excitement and danger of something new**.

Be in the moment.

Trust your inspiration.

And never try to repeat exactly what you did last time.

To help you explore this idea, imagine that whoever you are talking to is in **a different mood** each time you practise the speech.

- ○ Imagine they are in **a good mood.**
- ○ And then imagine they are **sad.**
- ○ Maybe you could imagine they are **distracted.**
- ○ Or **sleepy.**
- ○ Or maybe you could imagine they are **trying to interrupt you** the whole time.

Have fun thinking of **different moods** they could be in.

Then match your speech to *their mood.*

And let it influence the way you say it.

Taking the focus off yourself

Whenever someone speaks to someone else, they are usually trying to **have an effect on them**:

- ○ Maybe they want the other person to **really understand what they are saying.**
- ○ Or maybe they want to **teach them something.**
- ○ Maybe they want to get them **to agree to something.**
- ○ Or get them to **laugh.**
- ○ Or make them **feel guilty.**
- ○ Or make them **cry.**

There are loads of different ways people want to affect the person they are talking to.

So whenever you practise your audition speech, make sure you know **what effect you want to have** on the imaginary person you are talking to.

And try to connect with them!

> **I can't stress this enough.**

The speech is not about *you.*

It's about the *effect* your character wants to have on the person they are talking to.

Keeping the panel interested

My final piece of advice is probably the most surprising.

Your audition speeches may each be less than 2 minutes long, but even so **the audition panel can get bored!**

Oh yes they can !!

All the work you have put in to making your acting **truthful** and **creative** is perfect if you were performing the speech **as part of a complete play.**

But an **audition panel** has **no emotional connection** to the story and they know nothing about your character.

So you need to keep them attentive in other ways.

And there are a number of techniques you can use to do this...

Variety

Always keep truthful, but at the same time **look for variety in the speech.**

○ If a character is **shouting with rage** the whole time it can be **just as boring** as when they are **quiet and intense.**

Emotion

You will probably have found the **emotional changes** within the speech already but, if not, make sure they are **clear and defined:**

○ **Don't slide from one emotion to the next.**
○ Let each **emotional change** be stimulated by a **new thought.**
○ And then let it **spring into life.**

Rhythm

Try playing around with **different rhythms:**

○ Make some sections **a bit faster...**

○ And some **a bit slower**.

○ But let each change of rhythm **be definite**.

Mood

Similarly you can **change your character's mood**:

○ Find moments **of contrasting moods**.

○ If the speech is **sad**, find a line that might make your **character smile**.

○ If the character is **confident**, find their **moment of weakness**.

○ Find contrasting moods **that are suitable for your speech**.

Tone

You can make other changes by **altering the tone of your voice** on a line.

○ If the general tone of your speech is **sweet** and **romantic,** find a moment of **hardness** or **irony.**

○ If the tone is **heroic,** find a moment of **gentleness, romance** or **poetry.**

Volume

Volume is easy to change, and very effective.

○ You could suddenly **whisper an intense line**.

○ Or you could **shout for joy** if a particular line expresses your character's **happiness.**

○ Or you could let moments of **anger** explode.

Pitch

Similarly you can **raise or lower the pitch of your voice**.

○ Suddenly **deepening your voice** can often grab people's attention.

Pauses

Finally, see if you can **use a pause within the speech**.

If you suddenly **stop for a second or two** in the middle of the speech it can often make the panellists look up from their notes to see what's happening.

○ A moment for a pause is usually quite easy to find.

But of course you have to **fill a pause** with your **character's thoughts** to keep it alive.

I'm not suggesting that you use all these techniques in one audition speech, but if you **explore each of them when you are rehearsing your speech** you will be amazed at how useful they can be.

Remember:

> A change or two within the speech will keep the
> audition panel interested.

SHOWING THE SPEECH TO OTHER PEOPLE

Once you **feel confident with your speeches** it'll be time to **show them** to someone so you **get used to being watched**.

But still be cautious about showing it to **parents** and **friends**. They are not the best of judges.

At this stage a *negative* reaction could *destroy your confidence.*

And that's the last thing you need.

So find someone who is going to be *positive* about what you are doing.

If you are in a **drama group** or you have a good **drama teacher** you could always show it to them.

But still be careful.

They may know a lot about acting.

But they may not totally understand what is needed for a successful audition.

○ Ask someone you trust if you can **try the speeches out** in front of them.

○ Tell them that you want **honest answers**.

○ But tell them that you **don't want negative feedback**.

○ And you **don't want advice on how to make the speeches better**.

○ Tell them **you will *decide for yourself* how to make improvements**.

After showing them the speech, I suggest you ask them **specific questions**:

1. 'Could you **understand** what I was saying?'

2. 'At what point, if any, did you get **bored**?'

3. 'Did you fully understand the character's **emotional journey**?'

4. 'Was the speech **too fast or too slow**?'

5. 'Did I seem to be **communicating properly** with the imaginary character or audience?'

Let them be **a mirror for you to see your performance in,** but don't let them try to direct you.

You have to _trust yourself_ as an actor.

And do the speech the way _you_ think it should be done.

I'll say it again:

> **The best way of doing things is _your way._**

And it's the _only way_ to demonstrate your talent properly.

ADDITIONAL ADVICE

The 30-second preparation

All audition speeches are different, but your character **must have been doing something** before they start speaking.

○ Maybe your character was **walking down a corridor in a bad mood** before entering the room to speak.

○ Or perhaps they were **chatting to someone who has just left.**

○ Maybe your character has been sitting with someone else **trying to decide how to start a difficult conversation.**

○ Or maybe they have just fallen in love **and want to tell the world about it!**

You must decide what your character might have been **doing** and **thinking** for about **30 seconds** before they start speaking the words of the speech.

And then practise doing and thinking those 30 seconds.

So, let's imagine you are using one of the examples above...

First, **become your character.**

○ And then practise walking up and down outside the room for about 30 seconds **thinking about the things that put you in a bad mood** before coming into the room to say your speech.

○ Or take 30 seconds to **think through an imaginary conversation** with someone and only start your speech when you think they have left the room.

○ Try **thinking through your character's thoughts** for about 30 seconds as you sit silently with an imaginary person, until your character is ready to start the difficult conversation.

○ Spend 30 seconds **imagining the last few moments you spent with the person you've just fallen in love with**, and then turn around to start your speech.

These are just a few examples. You have to decide on something that is **suitable for your particular speech**.

> ### And then you should always do your 30-second preparation before launching into your speech.

The creative bubble

During your *30-second preparation*, imagine you are standing inside a **'creative bubble'**.

○ Everything inside the bubble is **truthful for your character**.

○ Keep all your thoughts focused entirely **within the bubble**.

○ Block out the rest of the world.

○ Inside the bubble, **you are your character**.

When you start your speech **stay inside the creative bubble wherever you go.** Let the bubble move with you.

And if you are talking to an imaginary person, make the **bubble big enough for them to be inside it too**.

Even bigger if you are talking to a whole audience.

○ Inside your bubble you are **a craftsperson at work**.

○ **Ignore the world outside your creative bubble.**

Letting your speeches unfold

Never speak your speech as if your character **has already decided what they are going to say**.

○ Let them **think through their ideas**.

○ Each **new thought** in the speech should be stimulated **by the thought before**.

○ Each **new phrase** should be spoken as if **it has just come into the mind of your character**.

○ The speech should be **a journey through your character's thought process**.

Something should change during the speech.

○ Maybe the character has **resolved some issues**.

○ Or **cleared their mind** of problems.

○ Or **discovered something new** about themselves.

An audition speech is not a static thing.

ANNOUNCING THE SPEECH

During the audition process you will be asked **what speech you are about to perform**.

1. Tell them the name of the **character**.

2. The name of the **play**.

3. The name of the **author**.

As in:

'I will be playing the part of (*the character's name*) from (*the name of the play*) by (*the author's name*).'

Fill in the names and **learn this sentence so you can say it clearly**, especially if any of the names are obscure or difficult to say.

(*Note: A speech from a well-known Shakespeare play should be announced slightly differently. The audition panel know that Shakespeare wrote* Romeo and Juliet, *so you can either leave Shakespeare's name out of the announcement, as in* 'I shall be playing Juliet *from* Romeo and Juliet', *or put it before the name of the play, as in:* 'I shall be playing Juliet *from* Shakespeare's Romeo and Juliet.')

From now on, each time you **practise a speech** you should always:

1. Start with **the announcement**.

2. Then do your **30-second preparation** while you set the chairs or move to your starting position...

3. And finally do the **speech**.

Follow this pattern **every time** you practise the speech so it all runs smoothly.

Then you will be in control.

And look confident.

Finally, remember:

You are a creative artist.

Many actors may have played the speech before.

But there is no 'right' way of doing it.

There is only *your* way.

And your way of doing it will always be the best.

3. IMPRESSING THE AUDITION PANEL

Having prepared your speeches and **sent off your self-tape,** you have now been offered **a live audition.**

Great !!

Reality check – There are about twenty major drama schools in the UK and each takes roughly thirty new students each year.

That's 600 people training to become actors annually!

Not counting people who have done **drama degrees in university** or have joined the **drama club while studying Ancient Greek at Oxford or Cambridge**!

A lot of people want to be actors because it sounds like a great job.

And it is.

But it's very competitive.

So if you want to be a ***brilliant*** actor...

A memorable one...

One that people queue up to watch...

One that has a satisfactory career...

One that gives you an income...

YOU HAVE TO MAKE SURE YOU STAND OUT FROM THE CROWD

AT EVERY STEP OF THE JOURNEY!

TALENT

Drama schools can teach you many things.

○ How to **use your voice properly**.

○ How to **examine a text**.

○ And how to **create a character**.

○ They can teach you the **difference between stage acting and screen acting**.

○ They can teach you how to do a convincing **stage fight**; **sing a song** with confidence; **improvise** truthfully and *dance the polka*!

They can teach you all these things and many more, but they can't teach you

⁓ TALENT. ⁓

And what is an actor's *talent*?

> **It's the ability to believe that you are someone else and to understand the world from that person's perspective.**

That's the talent, and if you don't have that you might as well stop now.

But you do have it, don't you?

Of course you do.

So when you audition for drama school you need to show them two things:

1. **That you've got talent.**

2. **That you are confident to use it!**

Those are the two most important things.

They'll teach you all the rest.

THE REAL X-FACTOR

Reality-TV singing competitions are very popular at the moment, and they have led people to believe that **the 'X-factor'** is the **ability to show off** and be **extreme in front of millions of people**.

The contestants often say they want **'to live their dream'**, and you see them **belting out songs** as they perform **pantomime versions of passion and sincerity.**

They screw up their faces.

Stretch out their arms.

Clutch their hearts.

And throw back their heads.

The judges say **they are going to be the next superstar** and the audience is encouraged to **scream with delight.**

You've all seen it.

But to my mind the performers, the judges and the audience have all forgotten what the word 'X-factor' **actually means.**

It's not about **skill.**

It's not about **showing off.**

It's not about trying to **live your dream.**

The *real* X-factor for a performer is that indefinable quality that makes people want to watch you.

That makes them feel connected to you.

That touches their hearts.

And lifts their spirits.

A performer with the real X-factor helps people forget their problems and takes them to a higher emotional level.

Do you see the difference?

It's not about *the performer.*

It's about the *effect* the performer has on *the audience*!

EMOTIONAL FOCUS

Watch old-school craftspeople at work. Someone who doesn't use modern electric tools.

○ Perhaps a **potter making something out of clay**, rotating the wheel with a foot-treadle as they shape their pot.

○ Maybe a **joiner** with just a saw and a chisel **carving the perfect wooden joint by hand**.

○ Or a **glass-blower** making a jug **by blowing down a long metal tube** into a balloon of molten glass.

When these people are working with these ancient materials they are not thinking about anything else except **the perfection of the object they are creating**.

And when people watch them there is **an awed hush**.

Nobody moves.

It's almost like being in a cathedral.

These craftsmen may not know it, but **they have** *the real X-factor*.

○ They trust their **skills**.

○ They have an **emotional connection** to their work.

○ They are **focused on their craft**.

○ And the people watching them **are captivated**!

So if you want the people auditioning you to be **totally captivated** by your performance...

You need to have an **emotional connection** to your acting.

PRACTICAL ADVICE FOR THE AUDITION

The 30-second preparation

When you are **performing your speech at the actual audition** it would be wrong to leave the room, or sit silently in a chair for 30 seconds, like you did when you were rehearsing.

○ But maybe you can find the time to think through the *30-second preparation* as you **walk up to the far corner of the room** before turning around to make an 'entrance'.

○ Or maybe you can do your *30-second preparation* as you **move a chair into the right position**.

○ Or **take off your jacket and fix your hair**.

But don't rush it.

This is your time.

And you need to do *whatever you need to do* to be at your best.

The audition panel will be impressed if you prepare properly.

But don't make them wait too long.

The creative bubble

Use your **preparation time** to come alive inside your **creative bubble**.

○ Remember that inside your bubble you are **a craftsperson at work**.

○ The audition panel is **outside** your creative bubble. Let them watch you, **but take no notice of them**.

Speaking to the audience

When your character is speaking to the audience don't forget that **your imaginary audience** would fill the whole room.

○ **Look around as you speak** so you are communicating with each and every imaginary person in the audience.

○ Make sure everyone in your imaginary audience **can hear you**. Even those at the back.

○ Make sure *they all* **understand what you have to say** (even though they are not there).

One more thing:

When your speech is to an imaginary audience

Never say it directly to the audition panel.

They might be **making notes,** or **discussing your performance** with each other, and that can be embarrassing for both of you.

So never look at them during a speech.

Look just over the tops of their heads.

TAKING OFF THE SAFETY BELT

One of the dangers of an audition is that you might **play it safe** and **not take any risks**. This may be okay, but your performance won't have the magic it had **when you were trying out new ideas at home**.

You will be like **a train running on fixed rails**, when you should be like

A dune buggy bouncing over unfamiliar territory!

So for your audition to be **exciting** you need to be in a *creative mood* when you are actually auditioning.

So practise being in a creative mood when you are rehearsing:

○ **Take off the safety belt.**
○ **Feel inspired.**
○ **And get used to exploring new ideas.**

And then have the courage to be in the same creative mood,

> Even when you perform your speech in front of the audition panel!

SIGHT-READING

Some auditions may include a sight-reading session. This is when you are given something to read **that you have never seen before**.

This could be **text** from a book, a **monologue** from a play, or a scene of **dialogue** from a script.

Text from a book or a monologue from a play

To practise sight-reading, **open any book at random and read out loud whatever you see on the page**. I would suggest you spend five to ten minutes each day doing this, so you get used to it.

○ **Read the text slowly,** pausing briefly at the end of each phrase or sentence to give yourself a chance to think.

○ When you take a brief pause, **silently read the next phrase or sentence in your head** before reading it out loud.

○ Make sure you **understand** what you are reading.

○ Try to **communicate the sense of what you are reading** to an imaginary person.

○ Have **an attitude about what you are reading** as if it was you who had written it.

○ Use your voice to **stress words that seem important.**

○ Don't worry if you stumble or make a mistake, **just correct yourself and carry on.**

A dialogue scene from a play or film

In order to practise sight-reading dialogue, you need to **read the text with someone else.**

○ The person who helps you **doesn't need to be any good at sight-reading.**

○ Or even have a clue about **acting.**

That doesn't matter.

When you are at the audition, **the person reading with you might not be good at sight-reading either!**

So learn how to make a scene **come alive,** even when there is **nothing truthful** coming back at you.

1. Ask someone to sight-read with you.

2. Have a copy of a play you don't know.

3. Open it at any page.

4. And read whatever dialogue is on the page with the other person.

When you are doing this, you should practise the following techniques:

- Try to **make a connection** between yourself and the person you are reading with.
- **Glance up at them as often as you can** without losing your place on the page.
- **Follow the text with your finger** so you can see where you are when you glance back down to the page.
- Try to **communicate the sense of what you are saying** to the other person.
- Try to **listen to what they are saying.**
- **Don't read too fast.**

Sight-reading is one of the skills that is often taught in drama schools, so all you have to do at the audition is **keep calm, use your acting skills,** and **do your best.**

But the more you practise, the better prepared you will be.

(Note: Sight-reading can be quite challenging for dyslexic people, but it is perfectly acceptable for someone who is dyslexic to ask for time to read through the text before starting. For more advice on reading strategies see: beatingdyslexia.com)

PREPARING A SONG

If they ask you to prepare a song they are probably just looking to see if you can **sing in tune** and have a **connection to the words.**

At this stage they won't be so concerned about the tone of your voice.

It would probably be a good idea to have a couple of sessions with a **singing teacher** if at all possible.

But if not, you can practise a few strategies on your own:

- **Choose a song you like to sing.** Not one you think the *audition panel* would like to hear.
- Choose a song that has a **decent tune.**
- Choose a song that **doesn't need accompaniment.**
- When you practise the song, try to **relax your body** so you don't look physically awkward.

○ Think about the words of the song and **sing them like you mean them**.

○ **Imagine the person you are singing to** and think of the effect the song will have on them.

○ **Enjoy the notes as you sing them.**

○ If you feel you are not confident about singing, try **talking though the words of the song,** keeping as close to the tune as possible.

○ **Use your acting skills to act the song.**

   (*Note: For a drama school audition there probably won't be an accompanist, but if you have rehearsed your song with a singing teacher or a pianist, you should bring your sheet music to the audition just in case.*)

A SCREEN-ACTING AUDITION

If a drama school wants to see you **acting for the camera** they may send you **a short piece of dialogue** to learn.

○ **Learn it thoroughly** and **practise it** with someone reading in the other character.

If they don't send you a scene, you should **practise your audition speeches** with screen acting in mind.

What's the difference?

There's a lot to learn about acting for screen, but basically it's as if the camera **can see into your mind**.

So be as truthful as you can.

Without being wimpy!

At a screen-acting audition it's a good idea to ask if they are filming you in a **close-up, mid-shot** or **wide shot** so you know how to judge the level and pitch the intensity of your acting.

Close-up

In a close-up your face is the only thing in the frame. Imagine that the camera can **see the truth in your eyes.**

- So try to eliminate anything that is a *demonstration* of emotion. **Just feel the truth.**
- Speak **quietly** and **intensely**. (*Unless the speech is supposed to be in front of a large crowd.*)
- Don't move about at all. **Keep your body still** and **don't move your head from side to side** if you can help it.

Mid-shot

In a mid-shot you are framed from **the top of your head down to about your waist**. The camera can still see the truth in your eyes, but it can also read **your body language**.

- **So allow your body to express your inner emotions.**
- Speak in **a normal voice**. (*Unless the speech is supposed to be in front of a large crowd.*)
- **Don't move from the place you are standing.**
- Allow yourself to have **natural facial expressions** that are appropriate for your character's emotions.
- And it's okay to **move your head** and **look around.**

Wide shot

In a wide shot the camera can see **your whole body**. You still have to be truthful, but you have the freedom to **move wherever you like** because the camera should be able to follow you.

- **Act as if the camera wasn't there!**
- **Trust the camera operator.**

And above all,

Trust your acting talent!

PRESENTING YOURSELF

Most drama schools will give you the opportunity to **speak about yourself** at some time during the audition.

This can be quite daunting.

Especially if you have **never been interviewed before** or have **never spoken in front of a large group.**

There are several things you can do to prepare for this.

An interview

When people are out of their comfort zone they often **develop defence mechanisms.**

○ They may appear **cool and casual**, as if nothing matters.

○ They may appear **overenthusiastic and talkative** as if they are exceptionally keen.

○ They may appear to have **a great sense of humour** as if everything's a laugh.

○ They may **retreat into themselves** and mumble their answers into their chest.

Perhaps you recognise your own defensive behaviour here!

But when professional actors are interviewed on television they usually look **relaxed and confident.**

_ Even when they're not! _

And why is that?

It's because they're _actors._

And they're _acting_ relaxed and confident!

So if you feel you are out of your comfort zone,

Start using your _acting skills_ to overcome it.

Interview practice

Try the following at home (you don't need to be with anyone).

○ **Sit comfortably in an upright chair,** resting your hands on your lap.

○ Don't sit up too straight but don't slouch either, just **make yourself feel at ease**.

○ Imagine there is another person interviewing you and **face them straight on.**

○ Then imagine they have just asked, 'Why do you want to be an actor?' and **answer the question out loud.**

○ Start telling the imaginary interviewer the reasons why you want to be an actor, making sure that you can **talk for at least 60 seconds.**

Maybe you have never been asked this question before, so it's a good opportunity to **gather your thoughts together**. Try timing it.

60 seconds is quite a long time.

○ Keep monitoring yourself for **any signs of defensive behaviour**, and if you are aware of any, **dump them and start again**.

○ Imagine you are talking to someone you are confident and relaxed with, like **your best friend** or **one of your grandparents**.

○ And don't forget to be **positive about yourself**.

You have just as much right to be an actor as anyone.

○ Check on how loud you are speaking and make sure that **you would be heard clearly** if there was actually someone there to listen to you.

○ **Use your own accent.** Don't put on a defensive streetwise accent if it isn't your true way of talking.

And don't try to be posh either. (Unless you are.)

Just be yourself.

(*Note: This brings up an important point. When people ask you questions in an interview they usually just want to hear you talk, to find out what sort of person you are. So it's important to sound positive.*

If they ask what shows you've been in it's no good just saying, 'I haven't been in any,' because the finality of that answer is deadening. Try to find a more positive response by saying something like:

'Well, as a matter of fact I haven't been in any shows yet, but I love watching films and I often imagine myself as the character in the film. Sometimes I even pretend to be the character when I'm walking down the street or going to the shops.'

or

'I haven't been in any shows but I love standing up in front of the class at school and reading out loud. I've always been good at doing different voices for different characters. Perhaps that is why I want to be an actor.'

*These are just a couple of answers that I made up. I can't tell what your experience is, but in both my examples I turned **a negative into a positive** and was able to talk for a few moments, each time revealing something about myself.*)

Here are a few questions that you may be asked in an interview for drama school:

1. Why do you **want to be an actor**?
2. Have you **done any acting**?
3. What **plays/shows** have you been in?
4. What character have you **enjoyed playing** the most?
5. Have you had any **actor training** so far?
6. What do you want **to achieve** as an actor?
7. Why are you auditioning for **this particular drama school**?
8. Who is your **favourite actor**?
9. What do you **know about this drama school**?
10. Do you **know anyone** who has been to this drama school in the past?
11. What **plays have you seen** recently and **who directed them**?
12. What did you **think of the acting** in a play or film you've seen recently?

Practise answers to **all these questions** on your own.

○ Make sure you are **positive about yourself without being madly over-enthusiastic**.

When you are confident with your answers, get a friend to interview you.

○ Ask them to choose questions from the list **in a random order**.
○ When you finish, **don't ask them to give you feedback**.

Trust your own judgement.

You will know instinctively if you did this properly.

Answering questions after your speech

You might be asked a couple of questions immediately after you have finished either of your speeches. Take this opportunity to show them that you are **confident and positive**.

○ Assume that they are **really interested in you**.
○ **Be pleased** that they have asked you something.
○ **Speak clearly and enthusiastically**.
○ **Look them in the eyes**.

Treat the person asking the questions as an equal.

These are the sort of questions that may be asked:

1. Where did you **find that speech**?

2. Have you **seen the play** that the speech came from?

3. Did anyone **help you with that speech**?

4. Do you **like the character in the speech** you have just done?

5. What was your **character's objective** in that speech?

Again, these are random questions, but it's worth practising your answers to them so you get used to the idea.

And always *tell the truth* at an audition.

If you get caught out on a lie you could easily *lose confidence* for the rest of the day.

And that's deadly!

Has the group got any questions?

Some drama schools gather all the auditionees together and **ask the group** if they have any questions.

Have a question ready so you can ask it. Here are a few suggestions:

1. What sort of **student accommodation** is there in the area?

2. **How big** are the classes?

3. How often do you do **one-to-one tutorials**?

4. Do **agents and directors** come to see the plays?

5. How long is an **average school day**?

6. Is it possible **to get a job in the evening or at weekends** or would that **interfere with the training**?

If you ask one of these questions don't just use the words I have written.

Think of your own way of asking.

CONCLUSION

I have given you some suggestions on how to work on an audition speech using your **talent** and your **imagination**.

And I've also explained how to practise **presenting yourself in a positive manner**.

You will be in **competition with other talented people** and your job is to ensure that at the end of the day **you will be offered a place at the drama school**.

It's no good just learning a speech and turning up.

You must have a professional attitude.

And you must convince the audition panel that you are the student they want.

This is your first step towards a successful and rewarding career.

SO IT'S IMPORTANT TO GET IT RIGHT!

4. THE DAY OF THE AUDITION

When you were rehearsing your speeches, some **amazingly creative ideas** popped up without you even trying, and they made your character come alive.

That's your talent at work,

And it feels fantastic.

Now you are going to enter the profession by revealing your talent to the outside world.

And that's exciting!

PRE-AUDITION TIPS

Brain, Body, Purpose

Here's something you can practise during the run-up to your auditions.

It makes you feel good about yourself.

Brain

- ○ Go outside and walk down the street.
- ○ As you walk, **look closely at everything you see**.
- ○ Examine the **cracks in the pavement**.
- ○ The **leaves on the trees**.
- ○ The **scraps of rubbish blowing** around in the wind.
- ○ The **buildings**,

the **people**.

Everything.

And as you do this, make sure you **have an opinion about each thing you see.**

Really get to know and understand the details of your surroundings.

And as you do this you will feel your brain come alive.

You will start to feel alert and quick-witted.

Yippee ! !

Say things to yourself like:

'My mind is as sharp as a razor.'

'I am witty and intelligent.'

'I could answer any question.'

'I can easily make people laugh.'

Concentrate on this for five or ten minutes.

Body

○ Still walking, shift your attention **down to your body.**
○ **Breathe in deeply** and **fill your lungs with air.**
○ With each new breath **feel healthier** and **stronger.**
○ Move your **shoulders back.**
○ **Expand your chest.**
○ Hold your **head up high.**
○ Feel like a **Greek god striding through the heavens.**

And as you do this, tell yourself **how good it feels to be alive.**

You could do any physical task with ease.

Let the adrenaline course through your body.

You are fit, healthy and strong.

Yes, siree !!!

When you are feeling at your best, say things to yourself like:

'I feel brilliant.'   'I could lift a ten-tonne truck.'

'I could swim the ocean.'   'I am ready to run a marathon.'

'I could scale the highest mountain.'

Concentrate on this for a few minutes.

Purpose

- ○ Now shift your attention down to your **feet and legs**.
- ○ **Lengthen your stride.**
- ○ Walk a **little faster** as you go.
- ○ Plant each foot **firmly on the ground**.
- ○ Stride with **confidence**.

And as you do this **develop a sense of purpose with each step.**

You know where you are going and you know what you want.

Your feet and legs will drive you on.

And your sense of purpose will get you where you want to be.

Oh yes it will !!!!

Say things to yourself like:

'I know exactly where I'm going.'

'My legs will take me where I want to be.'

'I can reach my goal just by walking.'

'I can go anywhere I want.'   'My sense of purpose will empower me.'

Concentrate on this for a few minutes.

Brain, Body, Purpose

- ○ Keep walking and **put all these three things together** as you walk.
- ○ Let your **brain** feel **witty** and **intelligent**.
- ○ Let your **body** feel **healthy** and **strong**.
- ○ Feel a sense of **purpose** as you walk.
- ○ **Brain. Body. Purpose.**

Keep thinking about these things **until you feel at your best.**

You can overcome any obstacle.

You can face any challenge.

Nothing will get in the way of you achieving your goal.

Jackpot!

Say things to yourself like:

'Nothing is impossible to achieve.'

'I can do whatever I want.'

'Nothing will prevent me reaching my goal.'

Practise this exercise as often as you like.

It will make you feel great about yourself.

Allowing your talent to shine

Your talent is a precious thing, and you have to look after it.

So during the final days leading up to an audition...

Make sure your leisure activities don't dilute your talent in any way whatsoever.

Here's what you should do:

Prepare your mind

○ **Get plenty of sleep.**
○ **Don't drink too much alcohol.**
○ **Don't take any recreational drugs.**

These things are vital. You need to have a **clear head** so you are **mentally alert**.

Prepare your body

○ **Eat proper food.**
○ **Get plenty of fresh air.**
○ **Do some exercise.**

This is **equally important**. An **actor's body** is one of the tools of their trade and it needs to be in **good condition**.

Prepare your clothing

○ Make sure you have the **right clothing** for the audition day.
○ Choose clothes that you can **move about in** so you are ready for any sort of workshop.

- ○ **Don't choose any clothing that is too revealing.** You never know what you may be asked to do. Make sure that you can **roll around on the floor without embarrassing yourself.**
- ○ **Dress as yourself. Don't try to be someone else.** If you usually wear jeans and a T-shirt, wear jeans and a T-shirt. If you usually wear dresses, wear dresses. Perhaps the best advice is to **dress the way that makes you feel confident.**
- ○ Whatever clothes you decide to wear, make sure they are **clean and in good condition.**
- ○ **Decide what you will be wearing in good time.**
- ○ **Lay your clothes out ready the day before.**

Prepare your speeches

I don't need to tell you to do this!

You've already done enough preparation!

You're ready and you know it!

THE DAY OF THE AUDITION

Don't forget that this is your day.

People are going to see you acting.

It's brilliant!

It's what you want to do for the rest of your life!

Getting up

Checklist:

- ○ **Set your alarm** so you wake up in good time.
- ○ **Have a shower** (or **bath**) and **sing a positive song** to make yourself feel alive. **Sing it loud.** ('Me' by Taylor Swift is good, or 'I Will Survive' by Gloria Gaynor if you know it.)
- ○ **Get dressed carefully.**
- ○ Have a **proper breakfast.**

○ Make sure you have **everything you need for the audition.**

○ Leave home in **plenty of time.**

Travelling to the audition

Right. So now is the time to use the 'Brain, Body, Purpose Exercise' (page 54).

○ Make sure you get **to the venue with plenty of time to spare.**

○ Find a street to **walk up and down** so you can **concentrate on the exercise.**

○ **Do it for a least ten minutes.**

Arriving at the drama school

○ As you enter the building, tell yourself **that this could be your home for the next few years.**

○ **Smile at any of the staff** that you meet and remember that **they need talented people like you.**

○ **Be friendly with other people who are auditioning.** Ask them about themselves.

Waiting to audition

One of the **biggest mistakes** you can make is to keep **thinking about the speech before you perform it.**

**If you have prepared properly, you don't need
to keep saying the words.**

You know them already.

So just relax.

**And only become your character when
it's time to audition.**

Workshops

An audition workshop serves **three simple functions**:

1. It lets the audition panel to see how well you **respond to instructions.**

2. It lets them see how well you **work with other people.**

3. It gives you the opportunity to **relax and enjoy yourself.**

The audition panel is trying to choose people **they want to spend the next three years with**. Of course they are looking for students with **talent**, but other things are also important.

- They need people who are **enthusiastic about the work.**
- They need people who **concentrate on the exercises.**
- They need people who have **plenty of creative energy.**
- They need people who **work well with other students.**
- **And they need people who have a positive attitude.**

So here's a bit of advice:

- **Listen carefully to any instructions.**
- **Do the exercise as described.** Never try to get their attention by 'doing it differently'.
- Allow yourself to be creative **within the confines of the exercise.**
- **Always be enthusiastic.**
- Allow **the people auditioning with you** to be creative as well.
- **Be positive about the work of other auditionees.**
- **Have fun with the group of people who are auditioning with you.**

One more thing. If you are asked to work in a **small group**...

- **Don't try to be the leader all the time.** Let other people have ideas.
- But don't hold back either. **Make sure you contribute some ideas of your own.**

It's important to get the balance right!

Bottles of water

- It's fine to bring a bottle of water with you, **but don't hold on to it all the time.**
- You may want to take your water into the actual audition in case your mouth gets dry. If so, put it **somewhere out of the way** but close to hand if you need it.
- Don't **hold it** or **drink from it** when the audition panel ask you questions.
- And never put a bottle of water on the table in front of the audition panel!

SPEECH TIME

At last, the opportunity to perform in public!

It's only a small audience.

You're acting on your own.

And the show is less than 5 minutes long.

But this is what you want to do, right?

So enjoy it!

You're bound to be nervous.

So you have to **turn your nervousness into excitement**.

Before the speeches

Follow these recommendations and everything will be alright:

1. *Turn off your mobile phone* – You don't want any interruptions.

   It'll mess things up for both you and the panel.

2. *Smile and look happy when you walk in the room* – Why not? It'll make people think you are pleased to be there.

   And you are pleased, aren't you?

3. *Don't try to shake their hands* – In other circumstances this is a polite way to say hello, but it's not appropriate at an audition.

   It looks like you're trying too hard.

4. *Let them take the lead* – They may be busy writing notes about the person they've just auditioned, so just wait patiently until they are ready.

   You could be upsetting their concentration.

5. *Don't ask which speech they'd like to hear first* – You should already have decided which one you would like to do first, so stick to that plan.

   Unless they tell you otherwise.

6. **Never ask the audition panel if you can speak the speech directly to them** – It's very off-putting to speak your speech directly to the audition panel, both for you and for them. **You may see them writing notes and think they're not listening properly.**

And that could really throw you.

Also, they may feel awkward writing notes when you are looking straight at them and that can **make them feel uncomfortable**.

And you don't want them to feel uncomfortable, do you?

7. **When they ask to see your speeches, they are putting you in the driving seat** – Up until now the people auditioning you have been in charge of the situation. They've told you where to go and they've told you what to do.

But the moment they ask to see your speeches they are **passing the control over to you.**

This is now your time.

And you need to do *whatever you need to do* to make your performance be at its best.

All the audition panel have to do is watch.

8. **If you need a chair, now is the time to ask** – You'll probably find that the audition panel has left a couple of chairs available for the auditionees to use.

But it's polite to ask if you can use them.

So why not ask them?

9. **Announce the name of your first speech only** – It can be very confusing for the panel if you tell them the names of the characters and the plays of both your speeches at the same time.

And you don't want to confuse the audition panel, do you?

10. **Don't try to fill them in with the background of the play** – They don't care.

They just want to see you acting.

Performing the speeches

1. *Do your 30-second preparation, just as you've rehearsed.*

   This should start to make you feel good.

2. *Get into your creative bubble.*

   This is exactly what you want to do for the rest of your life.

3. *Perform your first speech.*

   — Yippee-de-doo-dah! You're acting!

   So just let the audition panel watch the artist at work!

4. *When the speech is over, give yourself a few seconds to come back to reality* – If you snap out of your speech in a flash it looks as if your performance has all been on the surface.

   But please don't overdo the 'emotionally drained actor' bit.

5. *Announce your second speech and go through the whole process again* – Sometimes the panel will say something after the first speech, or they may ask what the second speech is going to be. Of course you should listen to them.

   But your time to be in charge isn't over yet.

   So if nothing is said, just move on to the next speech

   And perform it with the same focus and intensity as the first speech.

After the speeches

When the speeches are over, you can **hand back control to the audition panel.**

At this point several things can happen:

1. *They may ask you some questions about the speeches* – Be happy to tell them anything they ask for. But if you don't know the answer to a question, say something like:

   ○ 'I'm not sure. I hadn't thought about that before. What do you think?'

   ○ 'Sorry, I don't know. But it's a good point. I'll check it out.'

But never pretend to know something you don't.

2. *They may ask you some questions about yourself* – This is great.

    They want to know more about you.

3. *They may ask you to do one of the speeches differently* – There are only a couple of reasons why they might do this:

    ○   They want to see how you **react to direction.**
    ○   They want to see you in a **different mood or dynamic.**

    But one thing is certain...

    An audition panel *never* want to see you do your speech differently if they haven't liked what they've seen so far.

Think about it. **Why would they waste their time?**

So here's what you do:

○   Be **enthusiastic** about their direction.
○   Give their ideas **your best shot.**

Oh! And here's what you *don't* do:

○   **Disagree** with them.
○   Try to **justify** why you did the speech the way you did it.
○   Try to **prove they are wrong** by being half-hearted when you do the speech the way they ask.

Just remember:

They wanted to see more.

⁻ You should be very pleased with yourself. ⁻

(*Note: If a particular drama school asks you to do one of your speeches differently, they're not trying to improve it. They just want to see something different.*

So don't change the way you do your speech when you audition for another drama school.

Remember: your version of the speech is the best and only one you should perform unless a panel directs you otherwise.)

4. *They may just thank you and say nothing* – This means they've seen enough to make their judgement.

And there is nothing else you can do.

Leaving the room after the audition

Once the panel have indicated that they have seen enough, **never try a last-ditch attempt to win them over**.

If you tell them how much you want to be **offered a place**, or what a **fantastic audition** it's been...

It looks like desperation.

And it probably is!

So just thank them.

And leave the room with a smile.

AFTER THE AUDITION

Talking to other auditionees

After your speeches, you may be back in a room with the other auditionees and they might ask **how your audition went**.

But they don't care about you.

They just want to compare your experience with theirs.

So take no notice of what they say.

All auditions are different.

So if the panel don't say anything after the speeches it could mean that they thought you were *so brilliant* **nothing more needs to be said.**

Or it could mean they thought their training wouldn't be right for you and **nothing more needs to be said.**

Who knows?

If the other auditionees ask you how your speeches went **just tell them that they went fine.**

Even if they didn't.

Thoughts about the people who auditioned you

Don't forget, this is going to be **your training**. The people who auditioned you are probably **the people who will be teaching you**.

So after the audition process is over, ask yourself these questions:

○ Have you **enjoyed** the day?
○ Do you feel **inspired** by the comments of the people auditioning you?
○ Does this drama school seem to be an **exciting** place to train?
○ Could you be **creative** working with the staff at this school?
○ **Would this drama school suit your needs?**

You will be spending several years at drama school.

And you want to get the most out of it.

So choose the school that's right for you!

Recalls

After your first audition, you will either be rejected or you may be asked to come for a second audition. This is called a 'recall'.

Very few drama schools offer places after just one audition.

There are **many reasons** an audition panel might recall you:

○ Maybe they want **other members of staff** to see your audition.
○ Perhaps they want to **work with you** on your audition speeches.
○ Sometimes they want to do more intensive **group sessions**.
○ Or maybe they want to give you **a voice class**, or a **sight-reading test**.
○ Or perhaps they need to hear you **singing**, or **see you on video**.

Also they are probably thinking about the number of places they are able to offer.

But one thing's for sure.

If you get a recall, they have recognised your talent.

And they already like you!

Analysing how the audition went

After it's all over you will probably start to **analyse every detail of the day** and try to guess **how it all went.**

People sometimes get so stressed about the things they thought they did **wrong** that they completely forget **the things they did right.**

This is understandable, because an audition is really important.

But this is just **the beginning of a long career.** You still have a lot to learn. Nerves and inexperience are bound to affect you.

And remember:

Everyone who auditioned was nervous and inexperienced.

And the people who auditioned you take this into account.

So keep positive.

AND LEARN FROM THE EXPERIENCE.

If they don't offer you a place

Rejection is always hard to handle because **it can make you feel useless.**

But there are **millions of reasons why** you might not get offered a place and it's impossible to guess why!

So stop thinking about it.

Tell yourself they have made the wrong decision.

Go to your next audition with confidence.

And keep focused on your desire to be an actor.

What if you don't get into any drama schools?

You've got two choices here:

1. Give up.
2. Try again next year.

Well, you don't want to give up, do you?

So what do you do while you wait?

a) **Get a job** – You will need money when you eventually become a student so why not start earning some now.

b) **Meet lots of different people** – Think about their lives and how they view the world. It'll be useful when you are an actor.

c) **Do things you've never done before** – This will broaden your life experience.

d) **Go to places you've never been before** – This will open your eyes to other cultures.

e) **See as many plays as you can afford** – It will increase your knowledge of the profession (try googling 'Cheap theatre tickets under 26').

f) **Read plays** – If you can't afford to go to plays, then read some instead.

g) **Watch classic films** – Think about the acting and see what makes it interesting.

h) **Keep physically fit.**

i) **Read the news.**

j) **Have fun.**

And try again next year!

Lots of successful actors didn't get into drama school the first time they auditioned.

Next year you will be more experienced.

More mature.

And MORE DETERMINED.

SO NEVER GIVE UP!

PART TWO

GETTING ON

5. THE FIRST TERM

You've done it!

You're a drama student!

CONGRATULATIONS!

THE FIRST DAY

When you first start at drama school you will find yourself in a room with a mixed bag of fellow students. Maybe you haven't met so many people from different parts of the world before, or **even from different parts of your own country**.

- There will be people who have had **different educational experiences** from you.
- People from **different economic backgrounds**.
- **Different cultures.**
- **Different ethnicities.**

It's exciting but it can be a little scary.

The funny thing is, you have probably never been in a room with so many people who have the same ambition as you.

They all want to be professional actors!

So at last you have found a group of like-minded people who you will be spending the next few years with.

They are all just as *ambitious* as you.

They are all just as *optimistic* as you.

And they are all just as *talented* as you.

HELP !!

You will no longer be the **shining star** of your village, or your drama group, or your further education college – you are now going to be **a star amongst a galaxy of stars.** It can be quite humbling.

But don't worry just yet.

At the moment everyone is just as *nervous* as you are!

BONDING

During the first week you will start to bond with one or two of the other students.

○ They will probably be people who have a **similar background** to you.

○ Or have the **same interests**.

It's reassuring to make new friends. **It's fun.** It makes you feel secure in these unfamiliar surroundings.

So enjoy these new-found friendships.

But be cautious.

They're not necessarily the kind of friendships you need in order to achieve your ambition.

What?

Does that seem harsh?

Well, yes it is!

Acting can be a harsh profession and the wrong friendships can sometimes be too much of a distraction.

As a student actor you need to be equally committed to **two things** and you should explore each of them as fully as possible without letting them interfere with each other – they are:

The student life *and* **Your ambition to be an actor**

The friendships you make in the first few days will often be the ones to help you enjoy your **commitment to the student life**.

They'll be the people you want to party with!

Great!

This might be the only time in your life that you will be a student.

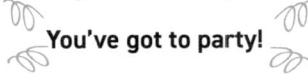

You've got to party!

Particularly in the first term.

You have to live the student experience to the full!

In fact, you have to live **all experiences to the full** because everything you do in your life will **broaden your understanding of human behaviour**.

And an actor needs that understanding.

So go for it!

But don't forget that you also have to **make the most of the training**.

You're going to spend several years with a group of talented students and you need to make sure you become the one who ends up with a **satisfactory and rewarding career**.

As the course progresses, another set of relationships will develop between people who have the same **commitment to acting** that you have.

The ones whose acting you can trust.

The ones who want to work as hard as you.

The ones who will rise to the top of the pile with you.

They are the ones who will help you **achieve your ambition**.

And with a bit of luck they will also be the people you want to party with.

And that can't be bad!

BANISHING DOUBTS

How can you make drama training really work for you?

That is the million-dollar question and it all starts now.

Pretty soon you will start the training.

- ○ Most drama schools will provide classes in *Acting*, *Voice*, *Movement*, *Singing*, *Dance* and *Combat*.
- ○ There may also be classes in *Improvisation*, *Devising*, *Shakespeare*, *Physical Theatre* and *Film & Television*.
- ○ And you may be studying the techniques of *Stanislavsky*, *Meisner*, *Ute Hagen* or *Lee Strasberg*.

That's a lot of stuff to learn, but these classes have one thing in common:

They are all designed to help you develop your talent.

Almost as soon as you start doing the classes you will begin to **compare yourself to other students**. Some days you will feel **confident** and **creative**, but on other days it will seem as if everyone else is **far more talented than you** and **you have no right to be there**.

But don't worry!

Everyone feels that way at times.

It's natural.

You are amongst a lot of talented people and you're not used to it yet.

They may all look **super-confident** but they are just as **unsure of themselves** as you are.

And they're hiding their nerves and insecurities.

Just like you hide yours.

In fact, they all think that *you* look super-confident.

The trouble is, when you watch other students in classes you find yourself **judging them**. And when that happens you assume that **they will be judging you**.

Which they probably are.

But this is early days. Some of the students who seemed brilliant in the first term never develop properly because **their commitment to the student life** is stronger than **their commitment to their ambition**.

And their talent gradually fades as the course progresses.

Luckily the opposite is also true.

A student who seemed a bit useless in year one...

Can sometimes blossom in year two...

And become the star of year three!

And that could happen to you if you commit yourself 100% to the course.

BEING LIKED

There is a good chance that **you want to be liked**.

In fact, people often become actors because they have a **real *need* to be liked**.

Actors get applause after their performances.

And it makes them feel good about themselves.

But here's a bit of serious advice.

The best way to be liked...

Is to like other people!

It's true.

So right from the word go make sure that you are friendly with **everyone**.

- ○ Let **the teachers** know you are keen on their classes.
- ○ Be enthusiastic about the work of the **other students.**
- ○ Smile and say hello to other **members of staff.**
- ○ **And always be positive about the work that the other students are doing.**

Believe me...

**If you let people know you like them,
they will immediately like you.**

Try it out.

It works brilliantly.

Job done.

BEING ON TIME

Here's an important piece of advice:

Never be late for anything.
EVER!

Why?:

1. **You'll keep people waiting** – Acting is a group activity. No one can start until **everyone is there.**

2. **You will be unprepared to work** – After rushing to get there you will be **anxious** and **out of breath.**

3. **You will feel rubbish** – Because you have **let everyone else down.**

4. **You will be annoyed with yourself** – Because you have **let *yourself* down.**

5. **The staff will label you as a bad timekeeper** – and that could affect **your casting in the final year.**

Yes it could!

Because you will start to get a reputation for being unreliable.

It's strange but true that the people who live **nearest to the drama school** are the ones **most likely to be late.**

○ They don't have to worry about **public transport.**

○ They don't have **traffic problems.**

○ And they sometimes **stay in bed** five minutes longer than they should.

○ Then they leave home **in a rush.**

○ And arrive late!

Here's some more advice:

Always arrive 15 minutes before your start time.

Then you can use that time to make sure you **are mentally and physically prepared to work.**

Listen.

You want to rise to the top of the pile, right?

Then never be late.

Enough said.

TEACHERS

Actors find it hard to judge their own acting **because they can't see themselves act**.

Of course they can **watch videos of themselves**, but even then it's difficult for several reasons:

○ **They concentrate on their own performance** rather than the interplay between the actors.

○ **They are worried about the way they look or sound**: 'My God, I'm getting a double chin, and my voice sounds awful!'

○ **They can still remember all their lines** so their performance doesn't sound as fresh and spontaneous as it does to other people.

These are **massive distractions** and they make it impossible to be objective.

So my advice is to avoid watching your screen performances **without the help of a teacher giving you feedback**.

As for your **stage work**?

Well obviously you can never watch that so you should **definitely** listen to the advice and feedback that teachers give you.

They can help you to see your work clearly.

And never forget that when a teacher gives you advice **they are only trying to help**!

I'll say that again:

When teachers give you advice they are only trying to help!

And again:

TEACHERS ARE ONLY TRYING TO HELP!

Why else would they become teachers?

DIFFERENT TEACHING STYLES

There are many different types of teachers and you may not like some of them, but **they can all be useful in helping you achieve your goal**.

○ So you should **listen to what they say**.

○ And **learn everything you can from them**.

Ultra-negative teachers

These are teachers who always seem to criticise your work.

They may think you are **extremely talented** but they never tell you that. They only pick on the things that they think **you're doing wrong**.

And this can be demoralising.

Especially if you are the sort of person who has doubts about your talent.

And who hasn't?

How to learn from ultra-negative teachers

Listen to what they say and **see if you can take their comments in your stride**.

○ Don't forget, you wouldn't be at a drama school if you weren't **talented**.

○ And you mustn't let your talent be **diluted** by negative teaching.

○ Keep telling yourself again and again that they are **only trying to help**.

○ **And keep believing in yourself.**

Ultra-positive teachers

These are teachers who seem to admire everything you do.

They give you masses of positive encouragement, but be warned. Their enthusiasm for your work may **make you complacent**.

'I'm great,' you may think.

'That means I don't have to work very hard.'

This is a dangerous trap.

How to learn from ultra-positive teachers

Listen to what they say and **let it build your confidence**.

○ Feeling **positive about yourself** is a good thing.
○ In fact, **confidence** is a major asset for a creative artist.
○ So **don't doubt** ultra-positive teachers.
○ But in the back of your mind, think to yourself: **'You may think I'm good today, but you wait... I'll be so much better tomorrow if I work harder.'**

Guru teachers

These are teachers who have a specific 'method' to teach.

They want you to sit at their feet and **hang on their every word**.

They believe their method is *the only way*.

But they have forgotten that there are many styles of acting.

And many different types of actor.

How to learn from guru teachers

Pay attention to their teaching **without becoming a loyal disciple**.

○ A specific method might feel like the **answer to your prayers**.
○ But don't become **fixated** on it.
○ That could **overwhelm** your own particular talent.
○ And **dilute** it!
○ **There is only one method that is right for you and that is your own.**

Lacklustre teachers

These are teachers whose teaching has lost its spark.

They have important things to teach but they have **been doing the same classes for too many years**.

You should feel sorry for them.

They have stopped being creative when they teach.

And they're bored with their job.

How to learn from lacklustre teachers

Keep focused and remember that they have **something important to teach you**.

○ Don't let their **lack of passion** rub off on you.
○ Let them see a spark of **enthusiasm** in your eyes.
○ That might **ignite their creative fire**.
○ **Teaching is a two-way street and a responsive student can often enliven and inspire a lacklustre teacher.**

Egotistical teachers

These are teachers who think that they are superior to the students.

They strut around like peacocks wanting everyone to admire them, but **they've forgotten the real purpose of teaching.**

They think that the classes are for *their* benefit.

And they're always seeking high status.

They especially love giving feedback because it makes them feel important.

How to learn from egotistical teachers

Pay attention to their teaching but **take control of the situation**.

○ Give them the **high status** they so obviously need.
○ Make them **feel good** about themselves.
○ Let them think you **admire** them.
○ If you do that, they may take the spotlight off themselves and **shine it on you**.
○ **Don't forget that this is your training and you must do whatever is necessary achieve your goal.**

Over-friendly teachers

These are teachers who want to forget the age gap and be your friend.

They like going to the pub with students and they love going to student parties because it makes them **feel younger than they actually are**.

But they sometimes get over-friendly with certain students.

Which can be difficult for the student involved.

And particularly awkward for the other students.

How to learn from over-friendly teachers

Never forget that you are on this course **to become a successful actor.**

- It can be very **flattering** when a teacher is over-friendly towards you.
- But you don't need that kind of **distraction**.
- And it can also be quite **destructive**.
- Particularly if they **turn against you** for some reason.
- **So if a teacher gets too friendly with you, back off a bit and let them turn their attention elsewhere.**

  (*Note: If any teacher crosses the boundary and makes an inappropriate, sexual suggestion, you should talk to another member of staff about it immediately.*)

Intense teachers

These are the kind of teachers who are very serious about acting.

They were often actors themselves, and probably very good ones, but they seem to be **lacking a sense of fun.**

They make profound observations about acting.

And they talk passionately about actors they admire.

They scrutinise your work with an intense expression.

And look deeply into your eyes as they talk about it all.

How to learn from intense teachers

They've got the **serious side of acting** right, but they have forgotten that acting is about having **a sense of play** as well.

- They want you to take your work **seriously**.
- So always **concentrate** in their classes.
- **And never mess about.**

- Otherwise they might **lose interest** in you.
- **Get intense with an intense teacher and you will learn a lot about acting.**

Eccentric/inspirational teachers

These are teachers who teach with a massive amount of passion.

We all love teachers like this because **they are fanatical about their subject.**

Their teaching is shaped by their artistic nature.

And they are continually having new creative ideas.

Unfortunately they often seem to contradict themselves.

And sometimes it's difficult to understand what the hell they're talking about!

How to learn from eccentric/inspirational teachers

Enjoy their eccentricity and **go with the flow.**

- Although their work can be mystifying, it's always **exhilarating.**
- Learn to appreciate their **passion.**
- Be inspired by their **enthusiasm.**
- And let them teach you how to be a **creative artist.**
- **They might not give you much practical advice, but they will probably be the teachers you remember for the rest of your life.**

OTHER STUDENTS

Students in your year group

When you start the course you will probably have **very strong opinions about acting.**

- You may **love the work** of one successful actor.
- But **hate the work** of another.

The funny thing is, you'll soon discover that other students in your year may **hate the actors you love** and **love the actors you hate!**

⚡ Weird! ⚡

To start with you will want your acting style to be **just like the actors you admire most.**

But as time progresses you will learn to appreciate **the different styles and talents of all sorts of actors.**

Until finally you will discover *your own style.*

But right now you need to learn how to work successfully with actors **who have different acting styles to you.**

And different working methods.

○ So be patient while other students **prepare to work.**

○ Accept their different ways of **analysing a text.**

○ Don't complain when they use different methods of **creating a character.**

○ Even understand that some students just **rely on their instincts.**

○ **And always help other students in their creative struggles.**

For the rest of your career you will be working with people who have **different ways of working from you.**

So get used to it.

Go with the flow.

And enjoy the differences.

Second-year students

During the first term you will probably see the second-year students performing and you might feel **quite critical of their work.**

But remember that they are only halfway through their training.

And most of them will be trying to overcome various technical difficulties.

○ Maybe one of them has **vocal issues** they are working on.

○ Or another has a **particular physicality** they are trying to improve.

○ Maybe someone has been **struggling with self-confidence.**

○ While someone else has been **trying too hard to impress.**

Another big problem that second-year students have is that they are sometimes given parts that are **not really suitable for them** in order to **broaden their range.**

○ This is a big challenge because they are forced to **explore unfamiliar territory**.

○ **And that takes a lot of concentration.**

Learning how to be a skilful actor is a bit like learning how to drive a car.

○ To start with, you are **awkward and hesitant** because you are not used to operating the controls.

○ But when the technical side of driving **becomes automatic,** you can **relax and enjoy the journey.**

Well, that's what it's like for second-year students.

They are awkward and hesitant because **they are concentrating on technical issues.**

But give them time.

And as soon as these problems are resolved they'll be able to relax and enjoy their acting once again.

So when you are watching second-year students, be careful how you judge them.

○ Talk to them and find out what they are **trying to achieve**.

○ See if it relates to **your own creative journey**.

○ Ask them about the **different processes** they have been through.

○ Find out about the **challenges** they've had to overcome.

○ **Learn as much as you can about their experience**.

They were in the first year not so long ago and they will love to talk about the training.

Third-year students

Your reaction to the work of third-year students may be quite different.

Their technique has become second nature so they can now **concentrate on giving creative and truthful performances.**

As you become more aware of the **challenges** an actor has to overcome, you may think that you will **never reach the same professional standard.**

But don't worry.

It won't be long before you are up there being just as amazing as they are.

Providing you continue to work hard,

and get the most out of every day of your training.

THE DANGERS OF PLAYING IT SAFE

Now that you're at drama school, it won't be hard to become a **good actor**.

But to be a *brilliant actor* takes a bit extra.

Technique classes

Most of the time, drama school training is **pure enjoyment** because it involves doing the thing you love to do.

> Acting.

But unfortunately some **technique classes** like *voice* or *movement*, or even *singing* and *dance*, can feel a bit boring because they involve a certain amount of **repetition** to develop **muscle memory** and **instinct**.

It's a bit like a musician practising scales every day so they can play their instrument without thinking about technique.

But you are your own instrument.

And you need to practise your exercises every day.

So you can act instinctively without thinking about technique!

If you want to be the student who **rises to the top**:

○ Stay **focused** in your technique classes.
○ **Concentrate** on the exercises.
○ **And develop a high standard of technical expertise.**

Acting classes

Acting is why you came to drama school, so make the most of these classes!

○ Sometimes you might be put into pairs to work on **short scenes**.

- At other times you may be part of a large group working on **a whole play**.
- Perhaps you will be asked to **devise a performance** from scratch.
- Or perhaps you will all be developing **improvised characters** in the style of Mike Leigh or Improbable Theatre.

It's fun.

It's creative.

And it's *exciting*!

And you will be exploring these things with people who are **just as talented as you**.

But this is where the **difficulties** lie.

- Some students will find the work **easier** than you.
- While others will **work harder** than you.
- There will be some students that **the teachers seem to like better** than you.
- And some who are **more confident** than you.

You're amongst a crowd of very talented people.

And you're just not used to it!

But so are the other students, and they all want to know **where they stand in the pecking order**.

And that's where the danger lies.

Everyone realises that they're being judged by everyone else.

- This may make some people want to **show off** to prove they are better than everyone else, and that could be **annoying**.
- Or it could make other people play it safe and **not take any risks**, and that would be **boring and uncreative**.

Do you want to be a show-off?

Do you want to be boring and uncreative?

Of course you don't!

So **stop worrying** about what other people think of you.

Never become a **show-off**.

Start **taking risks** right from the word go.

Challenge yourself to be dangerous!

Be the person who is most prepared to fail.

Then you will become the most exciting and creative actor in the group.

Just like the actors you admire most!

6. THE SECOND TERM

THE CHRISTMAS BREAK

Ever since you can remember, you have looked forward to Christmas!

So you will probably be excited to finish the first term and get back home to your family and friends so you can tell them **all about the course**.

But the trouble is, they won't understand!

This is because you are on the way to becoming a **professional actor**, and for most people acting is a **total and utter mystery**.

They have no idea how actors prepare.

And they probably don't even want to know.

But that's alright because acting is **the most wonderful magic trick** and it's spoiled if people find out how it works.

So over Christmas you will discover that **it's hard to talk to family and friends about your new passion**.

But also, long-term relationships sometimes end during the first Christmas break!

This is understandable because you have stepped into an exciting new world.

You are becoming a member of the acting fraternity.

And you share that passion with your **fellow students**.

They are becoming your **real friends** now.

Your tribe.

Your true companions!

These are people you will remember for the rest of your life.

And you'll love them because they are passionate about the same things as you.

So all in all, the first Christmas break can be a bit tricky.

RELATIONSHIPS WITH OTHER STUDENTS

As you plunge back into the second term with a feeling that you are drifting away from your previous life, **you may well start to have relationships with other students.**

That can be great in lots of ways,

But it can also be a problem.

In 'normal' life, people don't look deeply into each other's eyes and say 'I love you,' **unless they are actually in love.**

But actors often have to say these words to people they don't love at all.

And to make it feel realistic they use their own emotions!

This can lead to **complications, misunderstandings** and **genuine passion.**

You may fall in love.

You may fall out of love.

You may break hearts.

You may be heartbroken.

- ○ You may see the three-year training as an opportunity to have relationships with **as many other students as possible!** Some people do!
- ○ You may even find **your future life-partner** amongst the crowd you are training with! That sometimes happens!
- ○ Or you may be depressed because **everyone else seems to be in a relationship except you**! And that might be hard to handle.

All this can be a massive distraction.

Some people manage to **avoid relationships** with fellow students altogether.

But if you do **fall in love,**

> Have a **passionate one-night stand,**

> > Or experience a **traumatic break-up,**

> **You must never let it interfere with your training.**

> **Because that's why you're here.**

Drama school is a once-in-a-lifetime opportunity, and it would be stupid to waste it.

Falling in love

Falling is love is fantastic.

The rest of the world fades into the background and you are enveloped in **a rosy glow of mutual adoration**.

Your main objective is **to be with the one you love.**

> **But if you're not careful, this can cause a lot of difficulties.**

An acting course can be quite intense because students are sometimes asked to examine **their own emotions**.

> **And being part of the group becomes an important support mechanism.**

But when two students get into a relationship, **they don't feel they need anyone else**.

> **And this can have a bad effect on the whole group.**

So if you develop a relationship with another student:

○ Don't let yourself get **comfortably isolated** in your new romantic bubble.

○ Make sure you **keep close ties with the rest of the group**.

○ Leave your new relationship **outside the rehearsal room or drama studio**.

○ Make an effort to **avoid being 'couply'** when you're in the building.

○ Make sure **other friendships** are just as strong as ever.

○ **And party with the whole group just like you did last term.**

Falling out of love

When a couple breaks up, it tends to divide their friends as well.

○ Some people support **one person**.
○ And some people support **the other**.
○ Groups of students **whisper with each other** in the corridors.
○ And **friends become enemies**.

This can split a year group.

Obviously it's best if people who are falling out of love **keep the problems private and get on with their work**.

But my advice to **everyone else** is:

1. **Don't take sides.**
2. **And stay friendly with both people.**

It really is the best way because you can never be sure what went on in the relationship anyway.

So don't get involved.

The relationship is over!

It's none of your business anyway.

Breaking hearts

You may be the sort of person who likes to have **lots of relationships**, but please **have a thought for other people**.

You will be surrounded by **very attractive students**.

But don't have fun at their expense.

It could easily damage their training.

And yours!

So don't let *quantity* **be your main objective.**

Being heartbroken

If you get hurt, you may want to share your woes with other students.

That's fine, but **don't do it in school.**

- Meet up with your **friends**.
- Get **drunk**.
- **Cry** your eyes out.

But the next morning, put all that emotion into the training.

- Bury yourself in **your work**.
- **Learn** from the emotional experience.
- And turn a negative into a positive **by becoming the best actor in the group**.

You *will* get over it.

I guarantee!

MONEY PROBLEMS

Some people have **too much money** and some people **don't have enough**.

Both these things can be problematic.

No financial support

Some students have to pay their own way through the training **without any financial support whatsoever**.

This is the hardest scenario, but ironically it can also be the one that **results in the greatest professional success**!

Disadvantages

Working to earn money

- Without financial support you **have to find work** in order to **pay your rent** and **buy food**.
- You often have to work **every evening after school**.
- And you sometimes have to work **all weekend** as well.

It's very tough.

It takes up too much time.

And it makes you tired.

Drama training is usually pretty full-on.

Maybe 8 hours a day for 5 days a week.

The trouble is, drama students often have to do quite a lot of homework.

○ You have to **learn lines**.
○ Do some **research**.
○ Fulfil various **rehearsal tasks**.
○ And do some **written work**.

When you have to earn money, there is very little time to do that.

And the more homework you have to cram in,

the more tired you get.

So keep healthy and plan your day carefully.

Sharing a flat

Sharing a flat is great because you have a bunch of people to come home to after school.

The trouble is that some flatsharers may cause problems for the others.

○ Like not paying **the rent**.
○ Or leaving the flat in **a mess**.
○ Or playing music **too loud**.

All this can be a massive distraction.

Especially when you get in late from work and need to sleep.

But the opposite also causes problems. You may get on really well with your flatmates.

And it's always party-time in the flat.

So you want to party with the rest of them.

All night long!

And that can be even more tiring.

Not eating properly

Lack of money and lack of time can both cause you **not to eat properly**.

○ You often have to **grab opportunities to eat** between working and training.

○ Lack of time and money often results in you **eating rubbish food** because it's quick and easy.

But the training can be physically tiring.

And you need to get the right nourishment.

Otherwise you'll get ill.

Advantages

Believe it or not, the students who have to pay their way through the training are often **more focused on the work because they recognise the value of it**.

They are the ones who often **rise to the top** because **they hate working in rubbish jobs**.

And they want to earn their living as a professional actor when they leave.

Advice

○ Make sure you **eat properly**.

○ Have plenty of **fruit and vegetables**.

○ **Learn to cook a few basic meals.**

○ Make sure you have some **time on your own each day**.

○ Try getting to school **an hour earlier**.

○ Find an **empty room**.

○ Use this time **to learn lines, do research** or **catch up on written work**.

Some financial support

Some students are given a certain amount of financial support by **their parents** or through **a scholarship**.

This makes life a little easier, so they have more time to **focus on their training**.

Disadvantages

○ Even with some financial support, **flatsharing** and **eating properly** can be problematic.

○ You need to earn some money for necessities like **rent, food and clothing**.

○ This means you still **need to get a job**, although you probably won't have to work such long hours.

The extra free time might make it tempting to socialise more.

Which can easily tire you out.

And end up with you not working hard enough on the course.

Advantages

Students with some financial support don't usually have such large **financial obligations**.

Maybe they will only need to get a **weekend job**, or just work **in the evenings**.

This gives them a bit more time to focus on their drama training.

And having a job gives them a good work ethic.

So they are better prepared for a professional career.

Advice

Set aside a **certain amount of time** each day for the following:

○ Homework.
○ Eating properly.
○ Socialising.
○ Sleeping.

That will help you get on top of things.

You will get less tired.

And that will lead to more success on the course.

Time management is essential for students who have to work to earn money.

Living at home

Students who live at home don't usually have **to pay any rent** or **buy any food** so they are free from **most financial obligations**.

Disadvantages

If you live at home, you often have to make **lengthy journeys** to get to school.

○ **This can be expensive.**

○ And travelling each way can sometimes **take up a lot of time.**

Which makes the day very long.

Advantages

Students living at home **don't usually have to get a job.**

Travel time can be spent learning lines.

Or reading plays and theatre books.

This increases their professional knowledge.

Advice

○ **Leave home early.** Public transport is not always reliable so it is best to give yourself **plenty of time** to get to school in case there are any **travel disruptions**.

○ **Don't go home too late.** If you are having fun in the evening it can be tempting to put off going home **until the last minute**.

○ Make sure you **get enough sleep.**

Caring for a relative or child

Some students who live at home are actually **carers**.

○ That might mean **helping a relative to hospital** once a week.

○ Or **doing the shopping** for them on the way home.

Other students might have **children of their own**.

○ So they have to **collect them from the childminder.**

○ Or take them to **the doctors**.

Disadvantages

Looking after someone else has to be taken **very seriously**.

○ There is no possibility of you **slacking off**.
○ It can take up **a lot of your time**.
○ And it's very **restrictive**.

Advantages

Students who look after other people have to **take on responsibilities** when they are still quite young.

This gives them a mature attitude to the training.

And they take their professional career more seriously.

Advice

○ **Tell the staff and students what your responsibilities are** so they understand your problems.
○ **Explain your school timetable to the person you are caring for, or the childminder,** and let them understand how important your attendance at drama school is.
○ **Make a timetable of your duties** so you can compartmentalise them.
○ Keep strictly to your timetable so you can **fit everything in without stress**.

Looking after other people is a big responsibility for a student.

But so is the course.

And it's important to get the balance right.

Being a virtual landlord

Some students live in a flat that **their parents are able to buy** for them.

Which means they don't have to pay rent.

Disadvantages

○ Having few financial problems can lead to a **casual attitude about the work**.

○ Rooms in the flat are sometimes **rented out to other students** to help your parents pay the mortgage.

> **This can cause resentment.**

> **Which will make the atmosphere in the flat a bit tense.**

> **And that can interfere with the schoolwork that needs to be done at home.**

Advantages

Students with their own flat probably live near the drama school, so **they don't have to do a lot of travelling.**

> **They don't need to get a job.**

> **They don't have any major financial obligations.**

> **And they have more time and money to see plays and films.**

> **This increases their professional knowledge.**

> **And gives them a positive start to their career.**

Advice

○ **Be upfront about the financial arrangements.**
○ If you share your flat with students who are paying rent to your parents, **tell them exactly what your own financial arrangements are.**

> **It will be less likely to cause tension.**

○ Don't behave like a landlord.
○ Although your parents have bought the flat for you, make sure you **let your flatsharers have equal status within the flat.**

> **You are the lucky one.**

> **So don't let yourself become too bossy.**

> **The other students are paying to live there.**

> **And you aren't.**

Work harder.

> **Life is easier for you than for other students.**

But you want a satisfactory and rewarding career when you finish.

So make sure that you work extra hard.

BALANCING WORK AND PLAY

The second term is when you have to make a proper commitment to the training.

So never let your **social life** interfere with your work.

○ You can get drunk on **Friday night.**
○ Stay in bed till noon on **Saturday.**
○ Party as much as you like on **either of these days.**
○ **But take it easy on Sunday.**

Then you will be fresh and **ready for work on Monday.**

Every day you make a proper commitment to the training will put you **closer to achieving your ambition.**

And that's what you want, isn't it?

Remember:

The course is a lot shorter than you think.

So don't waste this fantastic opportunity.

Drugs and alcohol

Here comes the kind of preaching that some of you will want to ignore.

But listen.

Ignore me if you like.

Personally I have no objection to drugs and alcohol.

As long as they don't interfere with your ambition.

But if you do ignore me, **throw this book in the fire right now** because no other advice will help your career.

You will have already missed your opportunity.

Alcohol

Let's start with the legal one first.

A lot of actors have had a very successful career even though they were **a bit drunk every time they acted**.

It's true.

Alcohol releases the inhibitions and settles the nerves.

But I don't recommend drinking alcohol when you're working because you can get **a bad reputation** and that may interfere with **future job prospects**.

And how pointless is that?

My *strong* advice is to hold off the alcohol until after you've finished working.

Then you won't invite trouble.

Cannabis

Anyone who has tried cannabis knows that it makes you feel **relaxed** and **confident** and gives the world **a rosy glow**.

But anyone who has used it also knows that it **makes you paranoid**. And it also **affects your memory** and **changes your sensitivity to the passing of time**.

And both these things are essential tools of the trade for an actor.

○ Obviously **memory** is important because you have to **remember your lines**.

○ But the bigger problem is how **cannabis slows down your reactions**.

A good sense of timing is essential for an actor.

Cannabis messes it up.

Leave it alone !!

Also, cannabis stays in your system and affects your behaviour for several days after you've used it.

If you've ever taken cannabis, you know that's true!

Cocaine and amphetamines

These are very popular recreational drugs because they make you feel **confident** and **uninhibited**.

And who wouldn't want to feel like that?

But they also speed up your brain and make you talk very fast.

Unnaturally fast!

People using these drugs never **listen** properly when other people are talking, and **listening is a massively important skill for an actor**.

And if you're not listening, you can't react truthfully to what the other characters are saying.

You may feel as if you are acting brilliantly.

But you will *look* as if you are acting badly.

Psychedelics, opiates, legal highs, etc.

Drugs might be fun, but they are addictive and can ruin your life.

Why would you want to ruin your life?

You can have much more fun being an actor.

THE DANGERS OF NOT WORKING HARD ENOUGH

By the second term you will have settled down in the school and feel at home.

The course will seem to **stretch out for ages** and you'll feel that you can **relax a bit** and **take your foot off the pedal**.

Well... **you are wrong on both counts**.

○ In most drama schools the final year is devoted to public performances, so **the *actual training* is only two years long**.

○ So by the end of the second term you will be ***one third* of the way through the course**.

So make every day count.

The course will be over before you know it.

And you'll never get the time back again!

Don't take your foot off the pedal. If you do, other people in your group will go racing past you.

And they'll be the ones getting all the attention in year three!

Technique classes

By the second term you will have got to know the people who teach technique classes pretty well. And like all students **you will have discovered how to manipulate your teachers' weaknesses to your own advantage**.

○ You can be **slack with some teachers** and they won't be too cross.

○ You can be **charming with others** and they'll forgive you for not preparing properly.

○ You can even **mess about in some classes** and it won't seem to be a problem.

But what good is it doing you?

You may be **having a laugh with other students**, or **staying up late playing computer games**, but that's not going to help you have a satisfactory and rewarding career as an actor.

And what do you really want?

Your drama school training is an investment into your future life.

Invest properly and you'll reap the rewards.

And that'll be more fun than having a laugh or playing computer games.

Believe me.

So keep working hard in technique classes.

Acting classes

The problem with not working hard in acting classes is slightly different because **actors have to do a lot of homework**.

It's part of the job.

- There are **lines to be learned.**
- **Research** to be carried out.
- **Creative thinking** to be done.
- And various other tasks that **an acting teacher might ask you to do.**

If you *don't* do this work thoroughly you will feel the consequences when you perform.

- You will not be on top of things **but by then it will be too late.**
- You will struggle to remember your lines, **and no one can act properly when they're trying to remember what to say.**
- Your character will not be as interesting as you wanted it to be, **and you'll feel second-rate.**
- Your performance won't be truthful **and you'll feel like a useless actor.**
- You will start to panic in performance **and it'll be too late to do anything about it!**

Then you'll get unwelcome **critical feedback** from the staff.

And you'll know you deserve it.

The other students won't be enthusiastic about your work.

The staff will think you are lazy.

And that will affect their opinion of you for the rest of the course!

What a disaster!

You have come to drama school because you want to act, haven't you? Well this is an opportunity **you will never have again.**

At drama school you will continually be playing fantastic parts in brilliant plays.

And you won't even have to audition for them.

This will never happen in your professional career.

So make the most of it while you can.

Critical feedback

Throughout the course you will be getting feedback on:

- Your **acting.**
- Your **approach to the work.**

○ And your **general behaviour**.

Sometimes the feedback is **one-to-one**.

Sometimes it is **group** feedback.

And sometimes it is **written** feedback.

But never forget:

The only purpose of feedback is to help you progress successfully through the course.

Acting

Teachers are often quite critical of students who are **struggling with their talent**.

○ This is because they are aware of the struggle and want to help them **overcome their problems**.

On the other hand, teachers can also be quite critical of students **that they think are the most talented!**

○ This is because talented students often respond well to feedback and teachers can enjoy **watching them make improvements**.

So you can never tell what teachers think about the *quality* of your acting by the amount of feedback you get.

Approach to the work

Some students **rely too heavily on their talent** and don't feel that a lot of extra work is necessary.

But they are wrong.

All the most successful actors support their **creative instincts** with a **skilful technique**.

It's the perfect balance.

Teachers don't want the **naturally talented** students to fall behind the rest because **they haven't worked hard enough**.

So they can be very strict with their feedback.

But remember what I said:

The only thing that teachers want is for you to be successful!

You know that's true.

General behaviour

You may be **talented** and you may **work hard.**

But you may also be a total pain!

○   This is not going to help you with **your career.**

○   No one wants actors who **are a nightmare to work with.**

So if you get lots of feedback about **your behaviour,** it's only because teachers are continually trying **to help you become a professional actor.**

So listen carefully to what they say.

And take note.

When you have left drama school the only feedback you'll get about negative behaviour...

Is unemployment!

Getting very little feedback

There is only one thing to say about this:

If you don't get much critical feedback **it's never because the teachers have lost interest in you.**

It's just that everything is going according to plan.

And you're on the right track.

So just be happy.

Your response to feedback

The only suitable response to any feedback is to be pleased that the teachers are trying to help.

Say, 'Thank you.'

(Not necessarily out loud, just think it in your head.)

And then...

Make use of all their feedback in your future work.

7. THE THIRD TERM

The course started **just a few months ago,** but by the time you get to the third term you will have learned so much that **those first few nervous days will seem like some dim and distant dream.**

And yet there's so much more to learn.

There is a mountain to climb before you become a professional actor.

But you've already left base camp and you're on your way!

THE ART OF ACTING

Acting is an art form, and actors are creative artists.

Oh yes they are!

Sure, they don't use paints or musical instruments to create their art. They don't sculpt it out of stone or write it down.

Actors use their whole being.

And the characters they create are their works of art.

○ **Sculptors** understand how muscles and sinews shape the body – **actors have to understand their own bodies...**

And keep themselves fit and healthy.

○ **Musicians** practise scales and keep their instruments in tune – **actors need to practise vocal exercises...**

And keep their voices at the peak of performance.

○ **Painters** observe the real world and represent an artistic vision of it on canvas – **actors need to observe the real world...**

And represent their artistic vision in performance.

And that's the truth.

Acting is an art form without a shadow of doubt.

And by the time you reach the third term,

You are starting to become a real artist.

TRUTHFUL CHARACTERISATIONS

All through the first year you will probably be cast as **various characters** in scenes, films or plays.

You will be using **acting exercises** to create characters who are **quite unlike you**.

You may have been asked to play someone who:

○ Is a **different age** from you.

○ Has a **different way of speaking**.

○ Has a **different way of walking**.

○ Has a **different gender** or **ethnicity**.

○ Is from a **different culture**.

○ Was born in a **different era from you**.

These transformations were once the **essence of acting**, but **films** and **television** have now brought everything into **close-up**.

And most modern actors like to find **a deep truth** when they are acting.

So if they have to use **unfamiliar accents**.

Or **move their body** in a different way.

Or pretend to be **sixty years old**.

They often feel they are losing the truth of their performance.

Because they are not being themselves.

But there is a danger of being **so wedded to the truth** that **characterisations can become half-baked**.

Later on, you will be playing parts that are much more like you, but for now you should enjoy...

finding the truth in extreme characterisations.

○ Explore interesting **physical** and **vocal changes** while you have the opportunity.

○ Fully commit to the **externals of a character**.

○ And **find the truth in the *soul* of the character you create**.

During the first two years of training you have the opportunity to take the **biggest risks possible**.

And being half-hearted is not going to impress anyone.

Remember that the staff are always there to **guide you** through your artistic growth.

So make *bold choices*.

Enjoy your *successes*.

And learn from your *failures*.

Because failure is part of the learning process.

HOW DO I LOOK?

During this term, the **third-year students** will be meeting **agents** and **casting directors**, and you will start to realise that **an actor's physical appearance is an important part of the job**.

This can result in a **competitive atmosphere** amongst the first-year students to be **the best looking**.

So they do something about it!

○ **They work out.**

○ **Or they go on a diet.**

Both these things are obviously good.

The trouble is they can both be addictive!

Working out

Some students develop a **passion for being toned.**

They work out with weights in the gym.

This can be good for fitness and strength but **you can actually get too pumped up.**

And that might not be a good look.

Unless you are cast as a superhero!

Going on a diet

Eating the right food can keep you **healthy** and give you **lots of energy,** but some students **go on diets** because **they want to lose weight.**

○   This can possibly lead to an **eating disorder.**

○   And they might become **too thin.**

○   Because they are not getting **the right nourishment.**

A balanced diet is obviously good for you, **but don't stop eating healthy food.**

Otherwise you will become unhealthy and lethargic.

And your work will suffer.

Peer pressure

It's very easy to feel peer pressure to change the way you look.

But my advice is:

○   Do workouts to give yourself **stamina** and make yourself **physically fit.**

Don't do workouts to pump yourself up.

○   Adjust your diet to give yourself **energy** and to make yourself **healthy.**

Don't diet to lose weight.

Physical fitness and **good health** are both vitally important, but remember:

Actors come in all shapes and sizes.

And so do the characters they play.

> Whatever you look like, there will always be a place for you in the profession!

COMPARING YOURSELF TO OTHER STUDENTS

By the end of the third term, everyone in the group will have fathomed out **a pecking order of talent**.

- Some students will be **admired by everyone**.
- Others will be thought of as **less talented**.
- And there will be a whole **range of talent in between**.

You will be rated somewhere on the scale.

But ignore all that.

It doesn't matter what the other students think of you.

When you started the course, you were a **solo individual** in a room full of other individuals.

You have now become **part of a group**.

But remember that you are in charge of your own destiny.

And you are still a *solo individual*.

So don't let other people's opinion of you affect your opinion of yourself.

Be the actor you want to be.

It's the only way.

PREPARING FOR THE SUMMER BREAK

The summer break will be a welcome opportunity **to get away and have a holiday**.

Or get a job and earn some money!

But it will also be an opportunity to think about **what has happened so far** and **what is going to happen next**.

- Some things on the course will have **gone well.**
- And some will *not* **have gone so well.**
- So ask yourself **why that is.**

  It won't help you to blame other people for your failures.

  The only helpful thing is to look to yourself.

  And see where you went wrong.

So enjoy the break.

  You definitely need it.

  But don't waste your time.

- **Go to see plays and films.** Find out what is happening in the industry right now. This is the profession you will be trying to join in just over a year.
- **Re-evaluate your opinion of other actors.** Now you know more about the techniques involved, see if this has affected the way you think about different acting styles.
- **Read some classic scripts. Knowledge is strength.** The more you know about the history of the profession, the better equipped you will be.
- **Read books by actors.** Learn about their struggles and their successes.
- **Keep doing your voice exercises.** Your voice is your instrument. Keep it tuned.
- **Keep doing physical exercises.** An actor's body is a major tool of transformation. Keep it flexible and strong.
- **Eat properly.** Staying healthy is vital for an actor.
- **Explore new activities.** All the things you do in life become reference points for character creation.

But after a hard year, the summer is going to be a welcome break.

So don't forget to have some fun.

8. THE SECOND YEAR

Coming back into the second year is a bit weird.

Of course you expected the third-year students to have gone, but what is hard to get your head around is the fact that last year's second-year students have now become *third-year* students.

Surely they can't be good enough yet.

Not as good as the students who have just left.

But amazingly enough, they are. Because they have **learned a lot in the second year.**

Just like you are about to do.

But also there are now some new first-year students who seem incredibly young and nervous. And they are looking up to the new third-year students in **awesome admiration.**

Maybe they're going to be **disappointed in your acting** when they see you perform, just like you were disappointed in last year's second-year students when you first arrived.

There's a lot to think about here.

WORKING HARD

You're likely to be very busy in the second year because there is **so much acting to do.**

Technique classes will continue but there will probably be a lot more **plays** and **projects** that require:

○ Reading.

○ Research.

○ And rehearsals.

As well as:

○ Lines to learn.

○ And characters to create.

But acting is what you want to do, right?

So that's exciting.

The danger is that you may feel you **have learned so much** in the first year that **you don't need to work so hard** in the second year.

Some second-year students actually start to think that all the **text analysis** and **character study** they were taught in the first year was great, but it's just **drama school stuff**. So they abandon this work in the second year and think they can **rely on their talent and their instincts.**

They don't imagine that professional actors ever *action the text*.

Or create *objectives*.

Or think about *emotional memory*.

Well maybe they do and maybe they don't.

But *exceptional* actors do a lot more preparation than you imagine.

And you want to be exceptional, don't you?

Let me put this another way.

All the **technical stuff** you learned is what *exceptional* actors do *instinctively*.

You may have been taught a lot of techniques.

But they're not yet instinctive.

So you need to practise them more.

If you want to be the student who **rises to the top** you have to **practise relentlessly.**

And that takes hard work.

And total commitment.

(*Note: Any acting student who says they are trusting their instincts is like a car driver shutting their eyes because they think they instinctively know which way to go.*)

PLEASING THE TEACHERS

During the first year, the teachers were giving you **a lot of support** and **feedback,** and in the second year you maybe want to show them how much your **acting has improved.**

You want them to be pleased with you.

○ You want them to know that you are **committed to the work.**
○ You want them to see that your **vocal problems** have improved.
○ You want them to think that you're a **more interesting actor.**
○ You might even want them to think that you are **one of the best actors in the group.**

And all these thoughts get in the way when you are trying to act.

You start overanalysing your performance.

Even when you're actually doing it!

And that just makes things worse.

Because you now start thinking about how useless you are.

And you're still in the middle of a performance!

That's a nightmare, but it's understandable.

So here's what you have to do when you're acting:

○ **Forget the people watching you.**
○ Get into your **creative bubble.**
○ Build a **world of truth** around you.
○ And **never try to show how good you are.**

Just believe in the character you have created.

Get inside your character's head.

And let their thoughts be your thoughts.

Whatever you do, **never try to demonstrate** your character's reactions and emotions.

Don't *do* anything.

Just *think* correctly.

Believe in yourself.

And let other people watch.

STRIVE TO FAIL

Right, there is a lot of work to do this year, but it is also the last year when your performances **aren't going to be seen by the public**.

So it's your opportunity to push yourself to the limit.

This is vitally important.

The second year is the year to take risks.

So don't worry about whether you are a **good actor** or not. Worry about whether you're **a courageous actor** or not.

Nobody is interested in creative artists who play it safe.

○ Test yourself by making **risky decisions**.
○ Be **bold** in everything you do.
○ Find the truth in **extreme choices**.

And above all, remember:

You can learn a lot from your mistakes,
so don't hold back.

CASTING PROBLEMS

Casting problems are slightly different in the second year.

During year one, the staff were just getting to know you, so the **casting was probably quite random**.

But that didn't matter because the whole point was **to teach you loads of techniques**.

And to teach you various ways of creating a character.

Any character.

Year two is different because the staff know all the students a lot better.

- They know their **personalities**.
- They know their **strengths**.
- And they know their **weaknesses**.

So, wherever possible, year-two casting is specifically designed to help the students **on their journey to the third year**.

Expanding your range

Some students are fantastic actors, but they always want to play a specific type of character.

So to push these students into making bolder choices they are often cast in parts that are quite extreme.

- Maybe a **very old** character.
- Or a **flamboyant** character.
- A **violently aggressive** person.
- Or someone with a **big ego**.

Advice

If you are given a character like that, see **how daring you can be in your choices**.

Remember, this is for your own good.

Being extreme is not being untruthful.

There are a lot of extreme people out there.

And it doesn't matter if you fail.

Casting against type

Some students are only comfortable playing characters who are **very like themselves**.

- A student who's **loud** and **likes to dominate** may be given a **quiet, shy character**.
- One who is **dreamy** and **romantic** may be given a character who is **brash** and **thoughtless**.
- Casting against type **takes them out of their comfort zone**.

Advice

This is perhaps the biggest challenge of all because you are asked to **go against your own nature.**

Whatever you do, don't make the character just like you.

Explore the differences, however difficult.

Discover how other people think and behave.

And rise to the challenge.

Giving you confidence

Some students will be struggling with confidence at this stage of the course.

So the staff may cast them as a character who is **easy for them to perform.**

- O   This may be a character who has a **similar personality to the student.**
- O   Or comes from the **same part of the world.**
- O   Or a someone the student can **easily relate to.**

Basically, the student will be given a character that they will be able to play with confidence.

Advice

When you **enter the profession** you will probably be cast as characters **similar to yourself,** so don't knock it.

Explore your own emotional memories.

Use your own physicality and speech patterns when you create the character.

But also search for the differences between yourself and the character.

And enjoy the simplicity of the task.

Taming the ego

Ah-ha! This is an odd one.

Some students don't work well with other students because they are overconfident.

So the staff may give them a character that will help them learn to be part of a group.

○ They may get cast as a **minor character**.

○ Or someone who is just **part of a crowd**.

○ Or only has a **few lines**.

The student already has the confidence to play a leading role.

Now they need to learn how to share a scene.

Advice

Confidence is **vitally important** for an actor, so **be pleased that you have it**. But take this opportunity to learn how to be **supportive of other actors**.

Particularly those actors who have the main roles.

Make your character as interesting as you can.

But never try to steal the focus of the scene.

Give your attention to the other characters when they speak.

Never let your ego upset the balance of a scene.

And enjoy becoming part of a team.

(*Note: Fantastic actors always share the scene with the other actors. It's one of the things that makes them fantastic in the first place.*)

Making things fair

During the second year everyone needs the opportunity to **play something challenging**.

So the staff usually try to **balance the distribution of parts** over the whole year.

○ If you have had a couple of smaller parts, your next role could easily be a **leading role** or one that is a **big challenge for you**.

○ If you have just played Hamlet or Lady Macbeth, don't be surprised if your next role is **much less demanding**.

Advice

a) *Leading roles*

The responsibility of a leading role can be very tricky because that character **carries the weight of the whole play or film**.

Do as much preparation as you can before rehearsals start.

Forget about partying for a few weeks.

Be respectful of the other actors.

Share your character's emotional journey with the audience.

And don't forget to have fun with the role.

b) *Less demanding roles*

As the Russian theatre director Stanislavsky said: **'There are no small parts, only small actors.'**

A character with only a few lines in a play or film is still **a person with a full and interesting life**.

Use this opportunity to explore the unique qualities of your character.

Apply all your skills to make interesting and complex choices.

Give the leading actors as much support as you can.

Don't try to draw the attention of the audience if it's not appropriate.

And play the truth to the hilt.

The leftovers

There are roughly thirty students in your year and it is **nigh on impossible** to serve the needs of **each and every student** with **each and every piece of casting**.

The staff sometimes have to give a student one of the parts that was **leftover after the main casting was done**.

○ The part may not have been **specifically chosen** to help the student.
○ It may not be useful in helping a student **overcome specific problems**.
○ And the student may feel that the part **isn't a move forward** for them.

Advice

Don't worry about all this. It probably means that the staff think you are **on track** and **don't need to be pushed**.

But whatever part you are given, make it your own.

Enjoy the experience.

And give it your best shot.

You'll probably be given a more challenging part next time.

Other casting decisions

Who knows what the staff have in mind to **boost your talent** and make it presentable to the **professional world**?

Every case is different. But one thing is sure:

○ The ultimate aim of the staff is for you to have a **satisfactory career**.
○ They want that for **all the students**.
○ They have **your best interests** at heart.

Advice

Whatever part you are given in the second year,

Trust the decisions of the staff.

Face each new challenge in year two with enthusiasm.

And impress the staff with your commitment.

Take a positive approach to your work in year two –

It could have a positive influence on your casting in year three.

And ultimately that's what matters.

WORKING WITH PEOPLE YOU DON'T GET ON WITH

At drama school you are crammed in a **hothouse of learning** with a bunch of **young, insecure, competitive** and **stressed-out** people.

And none of you are used to it.

Acting is a very **emotional experience,** and when you are being creative you often have to expose your **weaknesses** and **insecurities** to other people.

That's not so bad when you are with people you trust.

But sometimes you have to work with a person you don't get on with.

Or don't even like much.

And that can lead to real difficulties.

So now is the time to **face up to the problem** and **deal with it.**

- ○ You can't be **friends** with everyone.
- ○ The most important thing is your **progress through the course.**
- ○ So don't let **personal differences** get in the way.

In order to be the person who is most likely to have a satisfactory and rewarding career, you have to keep asking yourself:

'What should I do to make things work best for everyone?'

I think there are several ways of approaching this.

Don't let your feelings show

There are always going to be people who **drive you bananas** for one reason or another.

But don't let them know how you feel.

This will **make everything a lot easier** for both of you when you **have to work together**.

Be supportive of other people

Drama school training can often make students feel **quite insecure**, and this can affect their behaviour and the way they work.

- ○ The best way to handle an insecure person is to **make them feel happier about themselves**.
- ○ **Never be critical of them.**
- ○ In fact, it would be even better to **give them positive encouragement**.

This will benefit both of you because **it will be easier to work together**.

Don't let any disagreements get out of hand

When you are working with other people, you **sometimes have a big difference of opinion**.

- ○ But a **constructive discussion** can be beneficial for both of you.
- ○ So **keep calm** and **listen to the other person's point of view**.
- ○ And never let an argument spoil a good **working relationship**.

But if things do start to get difficult –

Just back down!

What on earth does winning an argument matter? You just need to end up **being able to work creatively with other people**.

Control your own emotions

Sometimes you feel that you are **getting overemotional** during a discussion or an argument.

- ○ But if two actors have a row, **everyone loses**.
- ○ It creates a **terrible atmosphere** in the room.
- ○ **And the rehearsal falls apart.**

Then, later on, you start to **regret** your outburst and it **makes you feel miserable**.

So if you feel your emotions building up,

Just politely back away

And make sure you can calm yourself down.

Fighting to win an argument can often be destructive.

And what on earth does it matter if you win or lose?

Avoid getting into cliques

Sometimes you want everyone to know that a particular student **is getting on your nerves**.

- So you talk to **other students** about it.
- You want to get your problems **off your chest**.
- And you want other people to be **supportive**.

In fact, you want everyone to see the situation
from your point of view.

But that could easily **make matters worse**.

- The student who is getting on your nerves could think that you and your friends are **ganging up on them**.
- So they might start talking to another group of students **about you**!
- And that will create a whole lot of **tension between the two groups**.

So keep your opinions to yourself.

And don't involve other people.

Otherwise it will be nightmare for everyone.

Learn to apologise

This is a biggy.

If things get out of hand in your relationship with another student, **find a moment to apologise to them**.

Even if you think that they might be in the wrong!

You may feel that **apologising makes you weak**.

But in fact you are taking control of a difficult situation.

And you are helping to resolve the problem.

Your apology will make the other person feel good.

But it will make you feel great!

Bingo!

You've got a working relationship.

(*Note: The bottom line here is that you are using strategies to deal with relationship problems, and that will give everyone the chance of doing their best work.*)

Whatever you do, keep asking yourself:

Am I getting the most out of my training?

LEARNING FROM THE THIRD-YEAR STUDENTS

When you were in your first year you may have felt a bit intimidated by the third-year students.

**But this year's third-year students
are last year's second-year students.**

The ones who didn't freak you out at all.

In fact, you probably became friends with some of them.

So now is the time to learn from them.

Find out all you can about their experience of 'going public' **so you will be better prepared for it yourself.**

Things to ask third-year students about

The casting process for third-year productions

Some productions are cast using an **audition process**, particularly if the production is going to be directed by someone **who isn't a member of the staff.**

○ Find out what was **expected of the students** at their audition.

○ Ask how the directors **treated them.**

○ Find out if they **enjoyed the audition process.**

○ And ask them what they could have done to **ensure they got cast in a suitable role**.

Sometimes productions are cast by **members of staff** who know the students well.

○ Ask how the **casting was done**.

○ Find out if they could have **done anything differently** during their second year in order to be cast in suitable roles.

Working with visiting directors

These are **professional directors** who are hired specifically for third-year productions.

Visiting directors **won't know** any of the students in advance.

○ Find out what it's like **working with them**.

○ Ask how they **treat the students**.

○ Find out **anything that can be learned** from the experience.

It's important to know what to expect.

And how to behave.

Visiting directors may one day be in the position to offer ex-students professional work.

The experience of performing

During the first two years you have probably only performed to **members of staff and other students**.

○ Find out what it's like **performing to members of the public**.

○ Ask them what **they have learned** from the experience?

Working with the production department

You may not have worked with a **technical crew** before.

○ Find out what the technicians **were like**.

○ Ask if they were they **helpful**.

○ What was **surprising** about working with them?

○ What was **difficult** about working with them?

○ What was **expected of the actors**?

Other unfamiliar experiences

○ What are **costume fittings** like?
○ Or **wig fittings**?
○ Find out what happens during a **technical rehearsal**.
○ Or a **photoshoot**.

These things could be a distraction.

See if the third-year students have any advice on how to handle them.

Knowledge of the technical process will help you with your performance.

Meetings with industry professionals

Third-year students often get to meet agents and casting directors.

○ Find out **everything you can** about these meetings.
○ Ask them **what happens**?
○ Ask how **best to handle them**?

This is your career.

And you need to do everything you can to make it work.

So leave no stone unturned!

9. PUBLICITY

Next year, your acting talent is going public.

So some time during year two you're going to need to think about **marketing yourself**.

- Agents and casting directors will want to know **what you look like**.
- They'll also need to know what **acting experience** you've had.
- They want to know where they can see you **acting in the near future**.
- And they need to know what **kind of parts** you usually play.
- They would also like to see some **video clips** of your acting.
- And they would like to know how to **get in touch with you**.

That's a lot of information.

And they need it at their fingertips.

Your drama school will probably be contacting **agents** and **casting directors** at the beginning of next year with information about the productions your year group are going to be in.

So they usually produce an online yearbook or 'grad book'.

This will probably include a photo and CV for each third-year student.

This has to be ready by next **September**, so they will be working on it **during your second year**.

- You will need to get some **professional headshots** taken partway through year two.
- And you will need to **write a CV** detailing your acting experience.
- And it would be useful to start work on a **professional social media** site.

So this chapter is about preparing a professional marketing profile.

PHOTOS

In order to have your headshots ready for the yearbook, you need to organise a photo session **halfway through year two.**

Don't leave it too late or you'll get in a panic.

It can be quite expensive, so some students ask for a contribution to a **photo session** as a **Christmas present**.

Which isn't a bad idea!

Which photographer?

The right photographer for you is the one who takes a **picture that captures your personality.**

And that depends on the relationship between you and the photographer on the day of the session.

Of course, that's going to be **impossible to predict** unless you have had a previous session with the photographer.

But you can do quite a bit of research.

○ Look at **headshots of other actors** and find out **the name of the photographer** who took the ones you like.

○ Ask third-year students **which photographer they chose and why.**

○ **Ask a member of staff** for recommendations.

○ **Search 'photo sessions for drama students'** online.

○ Go to **photographer's websites** to look at the photos they took of other actors.

○ Find out who took the photos of actors who are **similar casting types** to you.

(*Note: 'Casting types' is an expression used in the profession to give directors and casting directors some idea of which parts will be suitable for you. It's hard to determine your own casting type but it would probably be based on your appearance, your background and your personality. Another way of looking at it is to think about the characters that are the easiest for you to play. Perhaps the best thing is to ask someone else what they think your casting type is. A member of staff, or a visiting director could help you out.*)

Costs

Photographers charge a **wide range of prices** for a session.

The more established photographers are usually the most expensive.

But not necessarily the best for you.

○ **A well-established photographer** – Their sessions can be quite formulaic because they have done so many of them, but they usually produce good-quality professional headshots.

But at this stage of your career it's not necessary to spend a lot of money on headshots.

○ **A mid-priced photographer** – These sessions will be pretty reliable and the quality of the pictures will be good. The photographer will be able to help you relax and be yourself.

If you can afford it, and you like the photographer's work, then this would be a suitable choice.

○ **An actor who takes headshots as a sideline** – With modern equipment actor/photographers can take some pretty good pictures. They understand how actors feel and what they want.

This session will be a bit cheaper and it'd be a pretty good choice at this stage in your career.

○ **An ex-student who is setting up a headshot business** – Again, the quality will be pretty good, but the lack of experience may be a problem. Have a look at some of their recent photos to help you make your mind up.

You may get this session at a reasonable price and the results may be perfectly acceptable, but it is a bit of a risk.

○ **A fellow student with a keen interest in photography** – They will know your personality very well, so that's an advantage, but their lack of experience could be a big problem.

This may be a really cheap session and the photographer will know your personality well, so it might be worth taking the risk.

And if the results aren't satisfactory at least they didn't cost too much.

○ **A family member or friend with a camera** – Try it if you like and you may be lucky. But don't expect to be able to use the photos **for professional purposes.**

Taking headshots for actors is an art.

You are about to become a professional actor.

So use a professional photographer.

Getting ready for a session

Your **face and hair** need to look good, so get **properly prepared**.

○ If your hair needs cutting, have it done **a week in advance** so it has time to settle down.

○ Finalise your decision about **what you are going to wear** the day before the session.

○ Don't **party** the night before.

○ **Get a good night's sleep.**

○ Wake up with **plenty of time to get ready**.

What to wear, how to look

There are three versions of you.

1. The way you **are**.

2. The way you **want to be**.

3. And your **casting type**.

Hopefully those three versions are **all the same** but, if not, you have to make a choice.

1. If you are unsure of your casting type, **the way you are** is probably the one to go for. Make sure you look your best without overdoing your make-up or hairstyle.

   Look smartish, but keep it casual as well.

2. Avoid **the way you want to be**. It's phoney. It's not you. And it won't help you get work.

   Don't try to be something you're not.

3. If you have a good understanding of **your casting type** then there is nothing wrong with bearing that in mind for a headshot session.

   But it can be limiting, so be cautious.

You could solve this problem by taking **alternative outfits** to the session or **changing your hairstyle** halfway through.

The session

**Some people love having their photos taken
and some people hate it.**

You've probably noticed that **in private life** most people do **weird things** when the camera is aimed at them.

They try to look like they're **having a brilliant time**.

Or they pull **funny faces**.

Or they **strike a sexy pose**.

Some people try to look **deadly serious**.

The way a camera lens stares at you can be **unnerving** and this makes people anxious about revealing too much of **their true personality**.

So they feel they have to *do* something.

But the most important thing for a professional headshot session is to **do nothing**.

Make sure you are confident and relaxed.

Allow the camera to see you as you are,

And let it *reveal* your true personality.

Preparation

○ On the way to the session do the 'Brain, Body, Purpose Exercise' (page 54) to get yourself in a positive mood.

○ Arrive **early**.

○ Spend time **chatting to the photographer** so you both get to know each other a bit.

○ Have a last-minute **check in the mirror** to make sure you look the way you want to look.

The session itself

The photographer is working during the session.

And just like you as an actor, photographers don't want anyone to notice the **technique behind the artistry**.

They may appear to be relaxed and casual, but there's **a lot on their mind**. They will be:

○ Choosing the **correct lenses**.

○ Making sure **the settings** are right on the camera.

○ Seeing how the **lighting** affects the shape of your face.

○ Checking that the **background** is appropriate.

○ **Framing** the picture correctly.

○ And making sure there is **nothing wrong** with the way you look.

But you won't notice any of this because a good photographer knows that **you need to be relaxed**.

○ So they will be **chatting** to you.

○ Having a **laugh** with you.

○ Saying positive things about **how you look**.

○ And telling you that you are **doing well**.

And you should be doing very little except **thinking positive thoughts**.

○ Chat with the photographer, but let them do **most of the talking** when they have the camera aimed at you.

○ Look into the lens and imagine you are looking into the eyes of someone **you are really fond of**.

○ Do what the photographer **asks you to do**.

○ Try to **forget** that you are having your photos taken.

○ And don't pose.

Don't grin.

Don't look intense.

And don't worry.

Just trust the photographer!

When the session is over, you may feel that you haven't done anything.

That's good.

It's the photographer who has been working, not you.

Choosing the right shots

A day or two after the session the photographer will **email you all the photos**. They will be **unedited** and probably **low resolution**.

Photographers offer a variety of deals, but you will probably be asked to **choose three or four pictures**.

This is hard.

At first glance you may **love all the pictures**.

But then you might have difficulty choosing any *you actually like*.

Or you may **hate all the pictures**.

And then the next day you may notice one or two that might be okay.

That's the way it goes.

Making your choice

○ Don't choose pictures that make you look **glamorous, sexy, intense** or **gorgeous**.

Unless you *are* glamorous, sexy, intense or gorgeous.

○ Choose pictures that make you look **pleasantly confident and intelligent**.

Someone who will be reliable and easy to work with.

○ Get some **advice** about your choice from someone you trust.

○ **But never ask family and friends for their opinion.** You are no longer the person they used to know.

You are now a professional actor.

○ And don't ask **too many people** for their opinion. They will all choose different pictures and it will just be confusing.

The best thing to do is to ask a member of staff.

They have a professional, non-biased opinion.

And let them do it **fast**, without too much discussion.

First impressions are the best.

That's how your headshots will be viewed professionally.

Editing the pictures

Photographers can do wonders with *Photoshop*.

- They can take out **blemishes**.
- Get rid of **wrinkles** and **bags under the eyes**.
- Make your face **thinner**.
- Make your eyes **brighter**.
- Alter your **hair**.
- And straighten your **teeth**.

But don't let them do too much.

Otherwise it will no longer look like you!

How long will these headshots last?

Actually not long.

You will probably be using them during the **third year** for **front-of-house publicity, Spotlight,** and maybe an **online yearbook**.

But as soon as you get an agent it is highly likely that they will ask you to get new photos done.

This first lot will be getting out of date by then.

SPOTLIGHT

Spotlight is an online casting directory of actors and you need to be in it.

- It's quite expensive, but it's **essential** to be on Spotlight.
- Spotlight offers a lot of advice for **graduating drama students** on their website, spotlight.com.
- They do a special **cut-price rate** for graduating actors.
- They also **offer advice and information** about all aspects of an actor's career.

Once you have completed **a year of full-time training** you will be eligible to join Spotlight, but **it costs money** and **won't be necessary until year three**.

When you eventually join **Spotlight**, you can include all your **professional information** in your **My Profile** page.

Media

○ **Headshots**

You can put a variety of headshots on **Spotlight** showing different aspects of **your casting type**.

○ **Showreel**

Drama schools often help each student with a **showreel**, containing clips from filmed work done during training. But if not, there are companies that will **shoot one for you**. These can be quite expensive though, so it may be best to wait until you have done some **professional filming**. You will update your showreel over time as you do more film/TV work.

○ **Audio clips**

The same applies to **audio clips**. You may choose to pay to have a voice-reel made so that you can showcase your voice for audio and voice-over work.

Casting details

○ **Location**

This is to inform casting directors of places where you have a base – i.e. **somewhere to stay**. If you have your own place and can also stay at your parents' place elsewhere in the country, that could be useful for them to know.

○ **Gender and ethnicity**

These are **purely for casting purposes**. There are a number of options for how you choose to identify and you can choose whether to allow your answers to be displayed on your profile.

○ **Playing age**

There is no need to put your **date of birth** on Spotlight. You are as old as you look.

It's far better to put **the range of ages** that you can play. The range should only cover 5 or 6 years.

'Playing age 18 to 35' is *not* useful information.

○ **Your height**

Height may be important for **casting purposes**. A photograph alone won't give enough information.

○ **The colour of your hair**

It may look **different in photographs**.

○ **The colour of your eyes**

The same here.

○ **Disabilities**

You can choose to add this information to your profile or not. Membership discounts for Spotlight are available for **deaf, disabled and neurodivergent performers**.

○ **Nationalities**

Include the name of the **country or countries** that issued your passport so that people in the industry will know **where you can work without needing a visa**.

About me

This is an opportunity to add information that will stand out to a casting director, such as **a brief note** about what you are **working on at the moment**.

The roles that you've played

The main part of your **profile** should be a list of **the roles** you have played and **the productions** you've been in.

○ The list should be in columns under the following headings:

Production, Year, Type, Role, Company, Director

○ If there is a role you are **particularly proud** of, you should put that **first** or **highlight it** in some way.

○ Otherwise you should start with the **most recent role** you've played and then continue the list in **reverse chronological order**.

○ **Film work** and **television work**:

This can include any low-budget **short films**, or **films** you have made in **drama school**. But always indicate what sort of film they were.

(*Note: If you haven't done any TV work yet, don't worry, that will be the same for most graduates.*)

○ **Theatre work**:

This can include any plays you have been in **during your training** but make sure you aren't **exaggerating**. You may have worked on a speech from *Hamlet* during your training, **but don't say you've *played* Hamlet!**

○ **Commercial work**:

Often an **actor's profile** will include a **list of commercials** so that commercials casting directors are aware of any **conflict of interest**.

(*Note: You probably won't have done any commercials yet so leave this out.*)

○ **Audio work**:

It's useful to include any **professional audio work**, but not a list of audio projects you have done as part of your training.

○ **Corporate work**:

If you've done any **professional corporate work** you may wish to include it in your profile.

Skills

Accents and dialects

You may have been taught a **perfect RP** (and you should mention that), but people in the industry need to know what your **natural accent** is because authenticity is sometimes vitally important for a production.

○ Don't write 'a good ear for accents'. That indicates that you're **not really perfect in any of them**.

○ Don't list the accents of **all the characters you've played** either. You may have got away with something that sounded like a Louisiana accent, but it probably wasn't perfect.

(*Note: If you eventually get cast in a play or film and they know the role isn't in your natural accent, they will probably employ an accent coach to help you.*)

Languages

○ If you are **fluent in more than one language**, write that in your **profile**, even if you speak other languages with an English accent.

○ If your parents came from different countries it's possible that you speak **two languages with perfect accents**. So include that information as well.

Music and dance, performance, sports and other skills

This section can include things like *presenting, singing, dancing, juggling, magic, playing the saxophone, horse riding*, etc.

But only include things you are **actually skilled in**, not things that you think you would probably be able to do if you had a couple of days to prepare.

Driving licences

○ Some touring theatre companies need actors who can **drive the van**.

○ Some TV or film roles need actors **who will be filmed driving**.

So being able to drive a car is a useful skill for an actor.

If you haven't already passed your driving test and **can afford to take lessons**, now would be a good time to **learn to drive**.

(*Note: Driving lessons would be a good Christmas or birthday present.*)

So get an up-to-date DRIVING LICENCE as soon as you can.

Training

Briefly mention where you **trained to be an actor**.

○ This could include a drama course in a **further education college** as well as your **drama school training**.

○ But don't include secondary school, university, etc. It's not important unless it included **specific theatre training**.

Only put in qualifications that are **helpful for people in the industry**, i.e. music grades, stage combat qualifications, etc.

Checking

Always **check the spelling** in your **profile**. It looks awful if you spell the name of a director incorrectly. If you're unsure about spelling, get someone else to check your **CV** for you.

Updating

○ As you get more experience you will be able to remove the stuff you did **before you came to drama school**.

○ When you get more **professional work**, you will be able to take out the **drama school stuff**.

○ As the years roll on, it is best to remove the **less notable professional credits**.

○ Finally, your agent may just be sending out a link to **your IMDb page**!

But that's a while off yet.

For now just make sure your 'My Profile' page is accurate, simple and clear.

And always keep it updated!

(*There is extensive information and advice about how to **complete and update your My Profile page** on* spotlight.com/help-and-faqs/updating-your-spotlight-profile)

SOCIAL MEDIA

Facebook used to be the most important social media site for professional actors to **publicise their career,** but at the moment **TikTok** or **Instagram** accounts are the favourite.

But anything to do with the internet is **changing so fast** that this could easily be different by the time you read this.

So ask the third-year students for their recommendations.

The internet is a valuable networking tool for professional actors.

○ So create a **professional** social media account.

○ Keep it separate from your **private** social media account.

○ Make sure that your professional information is **up to date** and **clearly written**.

○ Always let people know what **performances** you are involved in.

○ And keep in mind that the information is being **shared** with people in the industry.

PASSPORT

You may get a job travelling to another country **at any time in your career,** so it would be sensible to be prepared well in advance:

Make sure your PASSPORT is always up to date.

PART THREE
GETTING OUT THERE

10. THE THIRD YEAR

Things start to get serious now because **you are performing in front of the public**.

Agents, **directors** and **casting directors** (I'm going to call them *industry professionals* from now on) will be on the lookout for **new, young actors**, because the actors they signed up last year are **not so new** and **not quite so young any more**.

They're getting older.

So **industry professionals** love going to see drama school productions because it's exciting.

They might discover a new, young actor.

And that could be you!

And if you play your cards right, this will all be **great fun**.

So let's start at the beginning of the year:

CASTING

Over the first two years of training, the casting has probably been **shared out equally** so everyone has had a chance to **develop their talent**.

But things stop being quite so equal now!

Most drama schools try to give each student **a decent part** during their final year.

But it doesn't always work out the way you want it to.

Leading parts

It's just not possible for everyone to be given **a leading part** in the third year.

Think about it.

Too many students, not enough parts.

It just doesn't compute.

Of course, getting the main part is great.

- ○ It's what you **always wanted**.
- ○ It shows you that the staff have **recognised your talent**.
- ○ And **industry professionals** will have a good opportunity to see you acting.

Everyone wants to get the main part!

But having the main part also has **added complications**.

- ○ The **responsibility for the whole play** rests on your shoulders, and that is probably something you haven't experienced yet. **So you will be learning on the job.**

In front of an audience.

- ○ The audience will have **plenty of time to see your weaknesses** as well as your strengths, **so industry professionals** might start off thinking you are brilliant, **but as the performance continues...**

They may change their minds.

- ○ You may not actually have the **right temperament** for playing a leading part **and it will be a challenge to hold the play together**.

And everyone will see you struggle.

- ○ The **other actors** may not understand the **responsibility of a leading role**, so you won't get **the support you need**.

And you're out there on your own!

Supporting (or middle-sized) parts

To be quite honest, these could be **the best parts to have** in the final year.

- ○ You are used to having a limited performance time. **So you already know how to make the most of it.**

- The audience won't have time to think about your weaknesses. And if they like your performance **they will be left wanting more**.
- You can have fun creating an interesting character without having the responsibility for the whole play. **So the audience will be able to watch you enjoy your acting**.

Small parts

You can really **have fun** with these.

- There will probably be very little information about your character in the script. **So you can make the most of it by creating a character who is interesting and memorable.**
- You will have hardly any responsibility. **So the rehearsals and the performance will just be pure pleasure.**
- You can go onstage, make a big impact, and then leave the audience excited and happy. **And they'll remember you.**

Advice

If you are playing a *leading part*, remember to be an equal member of **the company**.

- Avoid being **aloof** and **distant** from the rest of the cast.
- Avoid being preoccupied **with your own problems**.
- **Help the other actors with their struggles.**

Working generously with the other actors will raise everyone's game.

Including yours!

If you are playing a *supporting part*, try to be **supportive**.

- Understand that **the leading actors have a difficult job** and help them in any way you can. **You may have the leading part in the next play!**
- Keep reading **the whole play** and make sure you understand why your character is in it. **Decide what your character needs to achieve.**
- If you have a scene with **one of the leading actors**, the scene is probably about **their character**. **Don't try to make it about your character** unless it is written that way.

If you are playing *small part*, remember that your character must be **important for the story** otherwise the writer wouldn't have written it.

○ Work hard on creating a **truthful character**.
○ Avoid a **clichéd characterisation**.
○ Always be **alert** and **ready to work** in rehearsals.
○ **Help the leading actors make the play work.**

Here's the truth:

It doesn't matter what size part you are playing.

If you do it well, the industry professionals will notice you.

That's their job.

RESPECT THE PLAYWRIGHT

Actors are part of a **storytelling team**.

And the principal storyteller is...

The playwright.

○ Make sure **you fully understand the story** that the writer is telling.
○ Work out **why the writer wants to tell that story**.
○ Do everything you can to make sure that **the story is clear for the audience**.

> That's the actor's job.
>
> It's as simple as that.

THE AUDIENCE

When you ask people **why they want to be actors** they often say things like:

'It's my dream.'

'I love it.'

'It's in my blood.'

They're saying that they want to be actors **for their own satisfaction**.

That it's all about them!

But the desire for personal satisfaction is like **an addiction.**

The more you have, the more you crave.

And you're always left feeling unsatisfied.

But I want you to consider **another reason** to want to be an actor.

Human beings are **tribal.** They need to be **part of a community.**

And the people who have the happiest and most fulfilling lives are those who serve the community.

It's true!

So in order to become **a truly great actor, one that people want to watch,** you need to stop being motivated by **self-interest** and start to realise that:

Your job can have an amazing effect on the people watching you.

The audience aren't **a panel of judges.**

They aren't **a crowd of adoring fans.**

They aren't **an enemy that needs taming.**

The people in the audience **are members of your tribe.**

And your purpose in the tribe is to **tell them a story.**

So do it for them.

Take the audience on an emotional and thought-provoking journey.

And they will love you for it.

THE CURTAIN CALL

The final ingredient to **make the audience feel good about themselves** is how you do the curtain call.

Here's what happens:

1. After a performance the **audience claps** to express their appreciation of the actors' work.

2. The actors receive the applause and **bow.**

3. This is **repeated several times** until the clapping starts to fade.

This is a **ritual**. But its purpose is **often misunderstood.**

When the audience starts to applaud, several things happen.

1. The actors **feel good** because the audience likes them.

2. So they bow to **thank the audience** for appreciating their work.

3. But when they **lower their heads** they are also **humbling themselves.**

4. And that means they are **giving the audience high status.**

5. And this makes **the audience** feel good.

6. The actors feel good. The audience feels good.

Everyone feels good.

So when you do a curtain call, don't just **bob your head up and down** without a thought. Remember **what this ritual is all about.**

And as you bow, think,

'**Thank you very much for appreciating our work.**'

THE TECHNICAL TEAM

During the final year of training you will probably be working with a **professional technical team** for the first time.

This will include some, or all, of the following:

- ○ **A production manager.**
- ○ **A set designer.**
- ○ **A costume designer.**
- ○ **A lighting designer.**
- ○ **A sound designer.**
- ○ **The stage management team and technicians.**
- ○ **The wardrobe department.**
- ○ **The set-construction department.**

And for film:

- ○ **A first assistant director** (aka 'First').
- ○ **A DoP** (Director of Photography – also known as a 'DP' or a 'Cinematographer').
- ○ **The camera crew.**
- ○ **The sound crew.**
- ○ **An editor.**

There's a **large number of skilled technicians** involved in the creation of a stage production or a film.

Actors are only a small part of a large collective team.

Student actors often fail to understand the **status** of the technical team.

But professional actors understand it, and they treat technicians **with the respect they deserve.**

The technical team are creative professionals.

They are not servants for the actors.

They are part of the team!

Treat them as **professional equals** and they will do everything they can **to make your performance a success.**

HOW TO DRESS

In year three you will be meeting **industry professionals,** so it's important to look the way that is most likely **to make people want to employ you.**

But beware! Industry professionals can pop up **when they're least expected.**

You may not be in the show that an agent comes to see, but **you might be in the foyer.**

- ○ The agent might spot you and **ask a member of staff who you are.**
- ○ The member of staff might then **talk about you** to the agent.
- ○ The agent might then decide **to come to see you acting** in one of the next productions.

And you may **never know** about any of this.

Until the agent wants to sign you up.

And then they may get you loads of work.

So whether you are in the show or not, the **way you look** when industry professionals are in the building is important.

So always make sure you look your best.

1. Don't try to be **someone you're not.**

2. Wear the clothes that make you **feel comfortable with yourself.**

3. And keep them **in good condition.**

4. Make sure your hair is always **the length and colour** you like it to be.

5. Clean-shaven, stubble or beard, make-up or not, it doesn't matter, **but keep your appearance just right.**

HOW TO RECEIVE PRAISE

After a show, people may want to **compliment you** on your performance.

That's great!

Assume they are **telling the truth** even if you were **disappointed** with your performance.

Why would they lie to you?

Accept the compliment with grace and humility.

Say 'Thank you.'

Don't let them know you thought your performance was rubbish.

They might start to agree with you.

HOW TO RECEIVE CRITICISM

It's tough. Friends and family are usually trying to be helpful, **but they don't realise how hard it is to perform in front of a large crowd.**

Actors are **totally vulnerable** in performance because their work is on **public display.**

They are fully exposed.

 Emotionally naked.

 And there is nowhere to hide.

Actors are fantastic because they do something that **most people wouldn't have the courage to do**!

 So if you get criticism from family or friends

 Thank them for their advice

And then totally ignore it.

 You must learn to be the judge of your own work.

(*Note: This applies to criticism from people not connected with your training. You should always take notice of **constructive criticism** from a member of staff.*)

WHAT ARE INDUSTRY PROFESSIONALS LOOKING FOR?

Okay, this is hard to take.

But it's good that you understand how the profession works from the start.

Most drama students have the **talent to act**, so it's not the first thing that industry professionals are interested in.

They talk about talent a lot, but the truth is slightly different.

Industry professionals are interested in three things when they are looking for student actors to represent:

1. **Casting type**

   This is the type of person you are, not your ability to transform!

   People in the industry tend to *typecast* actors. For instance, if they are looking for someone to play a Scottish character **they will cast a Scottish actor**! With so many actors available, why risk a Londoner doing a rubbish Scottish accent?

2. **Charisma**

   This is something beyond talent and a whole book could be written about it, but I'll try to break it down to a few identifiable ingredients:

a) *Confidence* – People like to watch actors who **appear to be confident**, because they don't feel worried about them.

b) *Enjoyment* – If actors seem to be **enjoying their performance**, the audience will enjoy it as well.

c) *Courage* – People admire actors who **take risks and do the unexpected**. It's exciting and gives them something to talk about.

d) *Personality* – The audience likes to see an actor's **unique personality** being a part of any character they play.

3. **Temperament**

This is not something you can demonstrate in performance.

It's how you come across when you meet people, or work with them.

Believe it or not, people like to work with people they like.

So when you meet industry professionals after a performance, in their office, online, or at an interview for a job:

a) *Be interested in the people you are talking to* – You may want to impress them by **talking about yourself**, but they will like you better if you **encourage** *them* **to talk about** *themselves*.

b) *Be enthusiastic* – A lot of people in the creative industries are insecure, so if you are **enthusiastic and positive** it will make them feel more **confident about themselves**.

c) *Be low-maintenance* – Successful actors are usually **easy to work with**. They never **cause a scene**, **waste time**, or bring a **bad atmosphere** into the room.

HOW TO TALK TO INDUSTRY PROFESSIONALS AFTER A PERFORMANCE

Equal status and mutual respect

When you meet an industry professional, remember that they have usually been in the business for a while, so you should **respect their experience and knowledge**.

But also remember that if an agent wants to talk to you after a performance it's because **they respect your acting talents**.

It's a mutual-respect situation.

But it's also an **equal-status situation**, because you each have something that the other person wants.

○ You want the industry professional's ability to **help you get work**.
○ The industry professional wants your **ability to act**.

You need each other.

Equal status and mutual respect.

Remember that.

Make them happy

Industry professionals come to see drama school productions as part of their job, **so if you help them enjoy their work they will love you for it**.

When you talk to them after a performance:

○ Be enthusiastic and **pleased to meet them**.
○ **Remember their name** and use it in conversation.
○ **Ask them about themselves**, not about their work.
○ **Chat about anything other than acting.**

Things to avoid (unless they ask, of course):

○ Avoid talking a lot about the **rehearsal process**.
○ Avoid telling them about the **acting techniques** you used.
○ **Avoid being negative about *anyone* or *anything*.**

Questions to avoid:

○ Don't ask them **who they represent**.
○ Don't ask them **how many clients** they have.
○ Don't ask them **what sort of work** they can get you.

And don't be negative about anything to do with your performance or the show.

Negativity is an unattractive quality.

They might say, 'You were great, but I didn't think much of the production.'

Don't say. **'No, the director was awful!'** Even if he or she has been a complete nightmare.

You don't have to lie. But you could say something like: 'The director was very demanding and some of the cast found it quite a challenge.' Then you could add, **'But I didn't have any problems at all.'**

Great.

You come across as a happy actor.

Talented and happy.

It's what everyone is looking for.

Believe me:

Positivity is a valuable commodity in the creative industries.

THE BOTTOM LINE

Treat the industry professionals as equals and make them feel good about themselves.

They will love you for it.

And when you're **successful** they will be able to say:

'I discovered her when she was still at drama school.

We became friends.

And I helped her get her career off the ground.'

11. GETTING AN AGENT

During year three, agents will be able to see you acting, either in public performances or on videos. If things go well, you may have a meeting with one or more of them. This meeting could either be in person or online.

This is an exciting time for both of you.

○ **You want to start work as a professional actor.**
And you hope an agent will be able **to introduce you to directors and casting directors**.

○ **Agents want to represent talented actors.**
And they've seen your work and **think you will have a successful career**.

(*Note: Most meetings initiated by agents are with student actors. Professional actors probably have agents already and it's considered unethical to 'poach' an actor from another agent.*)

TYPES OF AGENTS

There are many different types of agents and they work from a variety of 'offices'. More often than not these offices are out of town, so meetings are either **online** or at an **agreed location** in town.

○ *Large agencies* have *several agents* working for them. There will be a receptionist, **and each agent will have their own assistant and their own office**.

○ *Middle-sized agents* basically operate on their own **but usually have an assistant and/or a receptionist**.

○ *Small agents* often work from home or have a small office locally and either **work on their own or have an assistant**.

At this stage in your career it's impossible to say which would be the most suitable type of agent for you.

This is true!

But all agents need to make a living.

And the only way they can do that is by getting work for their clients.

SHOWCASES

Agents live **very busy lives** trying to get work for their actors, and although they love seeing drama school productions it's often more sensible for them to see the **drama school showcases**. They can see these in a **public performance**, but most drama schools now also provide agents with a link to a **video of the showcase**.

For a **showcase**, each student usually **acts in a short scene**. It's great for agents because **they can see a whole year group in about an hour**.

But this means that you have two specific tasks when you are cast in a showcase scene.

1. You need to play a character that is as **close to your casting type** as possible.

2. You need to make sure the agent can **see your face** when you are performing.

A showcase is a shop window for agents.

They need to get a clear idea of what they're looking at.

THINGS YOU NEED TO KNOW BEFORE A MEETING WITH AN AGENT

After an agent has seen your work, they will make decisions about several things:

○ Your **talent**.
○ Your **charisma** in performance.
○ Your **casting type**.

And if an agent has seen you in a live performance, and is **interested in representing you** they may wait around afterwards so they can get to **meet you personally**.

○ *They may ask a member of staff about you* – Agents learn to trust certain members of staff who tell them the truth about students and don't try to oversell them.

○ *They may introduce themselves to you* – An agent may want to chat to you after the show to get a rough idea about your personality.

○ *They may start 'selling' their agency to you* – The agent has seen your work and thinks you are talented. **But there are a lot of agents looking for talented students**. The agent may be interested in representing you but now needs *you* to be interested in being represented by *them*.

○ *And if all goes well, they may arrange a meeting with you* – The agent will probably want to talk to you one-to-one about how they can **help you with your career**.

This will be a *meeting*, not an *interview*.

And there is a **big difference**.

○ An *interview* is **when one person is trying to find out about the other person** by asking questions.

○ A *meeting* is where two people get together **to find out about each other**.

I'll repeat what I said before:

This will be an *equal-status and mutual-respect* situation.

Never forget that.

PREPARING FOR ANY MEETING WITH AN AGENT

This might be **in person** or **online**. It's possibly the first time you have had a meeting with an industry professional and you want to get it right because **it might be the start of your career**.

But you are in a strong position.

○ The agent has seen your work and **liked your performance**.

○ The agent thinks **your casting type is right for the agency**.

○ The agent has possibly talked to you briefly after a performance and **liked your personality**.

So now all you need to do is to...

Make sure the agent doesn't change their mind!

Research

Find out **as much as you can** about the agency.

○ **Go online** and look them up. Read everything you can.
○ Check out **the actors they represent**.
○ **Talk to members of staff** about the agent. They will often know quite a lot.
○ If the agent represents **any ex-students**, see if you can meet for a coffee so you can **ask their opinion** (*but be careful – if the ex-student isn't working they may be unreasonably negative*).

What to wear

I've already touched on this in the last chapter when I talked about how to dress when industry professionals might be in the building, and the same rules apply for a meeting, either **in person** or **online**, so I'll repeat them:

○ Wear the clothes that make you **feel comfortable** with yourself.
○ Keep them in **good condition**.
○ Make sure your hair **is the length, colour and style** you like best.
○ **Make sure you look just right**. Clean-shaven, stubble or beard. Make-up or not, it doesn't matter, but **keep yourself looking good**.

But I'll also add one other piece of advice that I think might be useful:

Dress the way that makes you feel relaxed and confident.

PREPARING FOR AN IN-PERSON MEETING WITH AN AGENT

Countdown to the meeting

- Make sure you know **how to get to the meeting.**
- Find out **how long it will take** to get there.
- Choose the clothes you want to wear **the day before.**
- Make sure they are **clean and in good condition.**
- **Don't party the night before!**
- Get to bed **early.**
- **Set an alarm** to give yourself plenty of time to get ready.
- **Have a good breakfast.**

Getting there on time

Now you are setting out to be a professional actor, you should get into the habit of **being early for meetings, auditions and rehearsals.**

It's annoying for other people to have to wait for you if you're late.

And why would you want to annoy anyone?

It's the same old story.

There is so much **competition in the profession** that no one needs to employ an actor who has **the reputation of being late.**

Plenty of other actors are good timekeepers.

So my advice is to get to meetings **15 minutes before the scheduled time.**

- Then you won't be **rushing to the meeting.**
- You won't be arriving **all hot and bothered.**
- You won't have to **apologise.**
- You won't **feel rubbish.**
- **And you won't put the agent off.**

More importantly:

You will be relaxed.

You will be in a positive mood for the meeting.

And you will impress the agent with your professionalism.

On the way to the meeting

Do the 'Brain, Body, Purpose Exercise' (page 54) so you are feeling **positive** about yourself.

Arriving at the meeting

Although you should get to the meeting 15 minutes early, **don't go in yet.** It's good to be early, **but not too early.**

○ The meeting might be at the **agent's home** or in a **tiny office**, and you will be interrupting them **getting work for their clients.**

○ The agent might have **middle-sized office** with a small reception area, and you might **get in the way.**

○ The meeting might be at a **large agency with a reception area** where other actors are waiting to be seen and **it could freak you out!**

So arrive at least 15 minutes early but then **walk around the block for a bit**, and press the doorbell **just 5 minutes before the scheduled meeting.**

That would be perfect.

Arriving in the office

If the first person you meet is **a receptionist** or **an assistant** then you should be open and friendly with them.

The agent may ask them their opinion of you after the meeting.

○ If the receptionist or assistant **looks busy**, just smile, **say something pleasant** and sit down quietly to wait.

- ○ **If they don't seem too busy** but haven't started a conversation, **start it yourself**, but make it general. Say something about the appearance of the office, or ask them if they live in this part of the city. Just general chat.

- ○ If the receptionist or assistant **wants to chat with you,** be pleased and enjoy the conversation, **but don't talk about anything to do with the agency.**

Unless they want to, of course.

Going in to the meeting

Your first entrance into the room is important.

- ○ **Don't barge in** like a whirlwind of ego-driven confidence.
- ○ But also **don't poke your head uncertainly round the door.**
- ○ Just **enter the room positively.** Stand up straight and look friendly.

If you **like to shake hands** with people, then that would be a perfectly acceptable thing to do. In fact, I would recommend it.

But if you are **uncomfortable** with that sort of greeting, **let the agent take the lead.** Shake their hand if they want to.

Being yourself

People will often tell you to just **'be yourself'** when you have a meeting with an agent, but that is quite a problem.

We all think we know who we are.

But we all behave differently depending on who we are with.

You probably behave differently...

- ○ With your **parents.**
- ○ With your **best friends.**
- ○ Or with a **teacher** at school.

And you definitely won't behave the same way with **a boyfriend or a girlfriend** as you would **if you met a famous actor.**

And think about the different ways you would behave **if you were at a festival** or **if you were stopped by the police**!

None of these ways of behaving are the same.

But they are all true versions of you.

So if you are going to meet an agent, which version should you choose to be?

Any of the above?

Not really.

○ You will probably be **nervous**.

○ You will obviously want **to make a good impression**.

○ You will want to show the **serious side** of your personality.

○ And you will also want to show your **fun side**.

I think perhaps the most suitable version of **'being yourself'** is the way you are when you **meet someone about your own age for the first time**.

And most importantly:

Don't treat the agent like a *schoolteacher*

Or your *parents*

Or your *best friend*.

Of course you need to let the agent know that you **value their professional experience**,

but you also need to let them know that you could **work well together**.

So the version of yourself should be *respectful*.

But it should also be *open and friendly*.

And never let yourself be **intimidated by the meeting**.

I'll say it again:

The agent has something you want, and you have something the agent wants.

You are professional equals.

So just enjoy meeting a new person.

What to talk about

When you first sit down for a meeting with an agent, all you are trying to do is **to get to know one another**.

But the agent already knows more about you than you do about them because **they have seen you acting.**

○ They have **liked** what they've seen.

○ And **they want to develop a working relationship with you.**

On the other hand, **you don't know anything about the agent** except what you might have discovered online or through conversations with other people.

So now you need to find out about them.

But that won't be difficult because **they will want to tell you.**

To start with, just remember:

○ This is a **getting-to-know-you chat.**

○ When they ask questions **it's not a test.**

○ All they want to do **is to open up a conversation.**

○ When *you* ask *them* questions, ask them about their lives, **not about their work.**

○ **Chat. Chat. Chat.**

○ **That's what it's all about.**

Subjects to chat about

Agents will be much more experienced in having meetings than you are, but they won't necessarily be any good at **having a chat.**

See if you can get them to talk about **anything other than business.**

○ *Where you were brought up* – Chat about **your home town.** See if they'll tell you about theirs.

○ *Drama school* – Chat positively about your **drama school experience.** They probably know some of the staff.

○ *Plays, films or TV* – Chat about **what you've watched** and ask if they've seen any of the same things.

○ *What you like* – Chat about things like **sports, food, music**, etc. See if you share any of the same interests.

Be interested in what they say and let their answers lead to more chatting.

- But don't chat about **your talent**.
- Or the **leading parts you've played**.
- Or the **fantastic reviews** you got in the local paper.

You don't need to sell yourself.

The agent already thinks you're talented.

That's why you're here.

You both just need to find out if the two of you can develop a good working relationship.

Funnily enough, you may find that the agent starts **telling you about their agency**.

After all, the agent knows you are **a talented actor**, but you have no idea **if the agent is any good**.

And they know that.

So they may talk about the **directors and casting directors** that they know, **the clients** they represent and the **sort of jobs** they will be able to put you up for.

This is useful information.

Particularly if you are going to have meetings with other agents as well.

It would be perfectly acceptable to tell them about **the sort of work you would like to do**. It's useful to be specific.

But if you are not sure, tell them you just want to work, **and ask their advice**.

Everyone loves to give young people advice.

Of course, there's nothing wrong with being ambitious, but **be realistic**. It's fine to say you want to make films in **Hollywood** or work at **the National Theatre** but you'll probably need to get a bit more experience first.

- So be **honest**.
- Feel **confident** about your future career.
- Talk to them about **your ambitions**.
- Have a **laugh**.
- **And be enthusiastic**.

Enthusiasm is an appealing quality.

What do agents want?

You may think that agents **are only in it for the money.**

But you're wrong. ⬅

Of course they want to make a **decent living.**

- But what they enjoy most is **being around actors.**
- They feel happy when they **make a deal.**
- And they love their clients **getting work.**

But they also get very excited about helping young actors at the start of their career.

That's why they've called you in for the meeting.

And remember:

The relationship between an actor and an agent is a professional partnership.

Agents don't get you jobs.

They get you interviews and auditions.

And it's up to you to get the job.

12. MEETINGS

AGENTS, CASTING DIRECTORS AND DIRECTORS

Here's how it works:

Actors employ **agents** to help them find work.

Directors employ **casting directors** to help them find actors.

So agents and casting directors are a professional link between actors and directors.

An actor has

An agent who introduces them to

A casting director who chooses suitable actors to meet

The director.

Five facts

1. Most **casting directors** will have a massive database of actors they have seen performing, **but they can't know them all.**

   So casting directors ask agents to give them recommendations.

2. **Agents** have a number of actors that they represent, but they need to find **suitable work for them all.**

   So agents ask casting directors what roles they are casting.

3. A good relationship between an **agent** and a **casting director** is extremely important for both of them.

   Because they need each other.

4. **Agents** usually get to know a few **casting directors** very well.

   They become professional friends.

5. **Casting directors** like **agents** who only recommend actors that are **suitable for the parts they are trying to cast**.

And remember:

Agents and casting directors love actors.

MEETING CASTING DIRECTORS

In order to 'beat the competition' you must make sure you are **thoroughly prepared for every meeting**.

Meeting a casting director who is a professional friend of your agent

When you leave drama school only a few industry professionals will know who you are, so your agent will want to **introduce you to as many casting directors and directors as possible**.

And casting directors need to be up to date with the new young talent.

So they will definitely want to meet you.

When you first join an agency you will probably have **several meetings** quite quickly as your agent introduces you to as many of their **professional friends** as possible.

These meetings may not get you any work.

But don't worry.

That's not the point at the moment.

The point is that the casting director needs to know two things about you:

1. What **sort of roles** you would be suitable for.

2. How you **conduct yourself** in an interview.

This second point is important for casting directors, because their **professional reputation** depends on the kind of actors they introduce to directors.

**And directors like working with actors who are
easy to get along with.**

But there's sometimes more to these early meetings than you can imagine. Here's what happens:

1. Your agent **contacts a friendly casting director** and says, 'I have just signed this brilliant new young actor. You must meet him.'

2. The casting director says, 'I'm casting a TV series at the moment. Unfortunately there's nothing suitable in it for him, but **why don't I have an online meeting to get to know him a bit**?'

3. Your agent tells you that you have a meeting with the casting director of the TV series and **you are excited**.

4. You meet the casting director and have a chat, but there is no mention of the TV series or **any parts in it for you**.

5. **Afterwards you feel you have done something wrong.**

But you haven't.

**Because there was never a suitable part for you in the
first place.**

**The casting director just wanted to find out more
about you.**

But **what happens next** is something you'll probably never know about.

1. Your agent then contacts the casting director and asks **how you came across in the meeting**.

2. The casting director tells your agent **what they liked about you** and **what were your weaknesses (if any) in the meeting**.

3. Your agent then contacts you, asks how the meeting went and tries to give you **some useful advice about future meetings**.

4. **Ba-boom!** Your relationship with the casting director has been established.

5. Your agent has **started work on your career**.

And if things have gone well, **who knows what will happen next month**.

Or next year.

Or even in a couple of years.

Casting directors have long memories.

Preparation

Find out **all you can** about the casting director before you have a meeting. You will probably be able to get a lot of information from your agent.

- What has the casting director **worked on in the past**?
- How did the casting director **start out in the profession**?
- **How long have they been** a casting director?
- **What kind of person** is the casting director?
- Apart from professional activities, **what other interests does the casting director have** (sports, holidays, socialising, etc.)?

The meeting itself

The important thing to remember is that casting directors are human and **human beings enjoy positive contact with each other**.

The more you are able to contribute towards **an enjoyable meeting**, the more likelihood there will be of them keeping you at **the top of their list** for future casting opportunities.

- So treat this meeting like a **social occasion** when two people are trying to get to know each other.

    And assume that the casting director is going to like you.

- You don't have to persuade the Casting Director that you are talented.

    Your agent thinks you're talented.

    And the casting director trusts your agent.

- You don't have to pretend to be someone you are not.

    The casting director wants to know what you're *actually like*.

    So just relax.

- **Chat about things.**

    You both have an interest in theatre and films.

    Or you can talk about the reality-TV shows.

    Or things that are going on in the world.

○ But be honest about your opinions.

And enjoy meeting someone new.

(*Note: For a meeting like this it is best to avoid talking about contentious issues like politics or religion. There is no point in getting into a conversation where you end up with a major difference of opinion.*)

Meeting a casting director or a director for a specific role

Sometimes the first step towards **getting a particular role** is a meeting with just the casting director.

Particularly on **big-budget projects**, when the casting director wants to see **lots of actors** for each role but only selects **a small number** of them to meet the director.

Preparation

If you're going to have a meeting with a casting director or a director that you don't know, **ask your agent about them**.

The more **information** you have about the people you meet, the more **relaxed** you will be when you talk to them.

○ Find out all you can about **the director and their work**.

○ Find out all you can about **the job/company/organisation/film/play, etc.**

If you want to beat the competition, you need to be able to **talk as knowledgeably about the project as you can**.

○ So if it's a role in a published play, **read the play thoroughly. Several times.**

○ If you are sent an unpublished script, **read the script thoroughly. Several times.**

○ If the script is an adaptation of a novel, **read the novel** – the interview may only be a couple of days away but *start* **reading the novel.** Then at least you will be able to talk about the first few chapters.

○ If you are asked to look at a particular scene, **memorise it.**

The director is more likely to want to work with you if the two of you can have a proper conversation about the project.

Now here's a very important bit of preparation:

Make sure you know your own CV.

This may sound obvious, but it's surprising how **your mind goes blank** when you are in an important meeting.

So remind yourself of **what you've done** and **who you've worked with**.

○ **The plays or films** you have been in.
○ The names of **the people who wrote them.**
○ The names of **the characters you've played.**
○ The names of **the actors you've worked with.**
○ **And the names of the people who've directed you.**

If someone asks you the name of a **director** you worked with last year, or the name of the person who **wrote the play you were in**, and you can't remember what they were called, **you will panic and feel useless.**

And then you will lose confidence in yourself.

And that could spoil your chances of getting the job.

So this is not a joke.

I'll say it again:

Make sure you know your own CV.

The meeting itself

The most important thing to remind yourself is that **you, the director and the casting director are all *professional equals*.**

Each person has something that the others want.

1. The director has a **job to offer**.

And you want it.

2. The casting director has a **database of actors**.

And the director wants to be presented with a selection of suitable actors for their project.

3. You have the **talent and skill to act**.

And the director and the casting director both want talented actors.

Let me make this clear.

Not everyone can act.

And **high-quality drama** for theatre, film and television needs **talented actors**.

Actors are a valuable commodity.

> *You* are a valuable commodity.

Never forget that.

Here are a few things to consider when meeting a director or a casting director:

The first few moments

(I've said it before) **Assume they will like you** – why wouldn't they? They want to work with people they like.

And you want that too.

○ Start the meeting feeling **positive about yourself**.

(*Note: If it's an in-person meeting, don't poke your head around the door as if you're not worthy, but on the other hand don't stride in like you own the place.*)

Look confident without being arrogant.

○ Let them know that you are **pleased to have the meeting** – they will want you to like them just as much as you want them to like you.

They're human beings after all.

○ If anyone in the meeting tells you their name, **make sure you remember it** so you can use it sparingly throughout.

People feel good when other people use their name.

○ Take a few moments for social chat, **but keep it short and positive** – the first few minutes of any meeting need to be relaxed and casual before you get down to business.

But beware of chattering on for ages.

○ Create a good atmosphere with humour and intelligence – again, this needs to be properly balanced.

Not too jokey and not too intense.

The conversation

An in-person meeting

The simple advice for an in-person meeting is:

Sit up straight.

Maintain a natural eye contact.

And breathe.

Never forget that you are an **interesting and talented actor**.

If you have the opportunity to work with someone **role-playing a director**, then you could practise the following:

○ **Sit comfortably.**

Don't slump in your chair as if you don't care, but on the other hand don't perch on the edge because it will make you look tense and unrelaxed.

○ **Mirror the body language of the person you are talking to.**

If they look relaxed and comfortable then you should too. If they look alert and businesslike then that would be a good way for you to look.

○ **Pace the conversation.**

Speaking too fast makes you look nervous, and speaking too slow makes it look as if you don't care.

○ **Make eye contact.**

Look them in the eye when you talk to them, but don't stare too much. And whatever you do, don't look down at the floor or stare at your hands. And definitely don't gaze around the room.

○ **Share your attention.**

Don't leave anyone out of the conversation. Keep your main focus on the director, but make regular eye contact with any other people in the room as you talk.

An online meeting

○ Look at the camera lens when you are speaking, not the screen.

All meetings

○ **Pay careful attention to what is being said.**

Sometimes there is so much going on in your mind that **you don't listen**

carefully when people speak. But the details may be important later on, so make sure you really focus on what you are being told.

○ **Let them talk.**

The project is important to them, so they may want to tell you all about it. **Concentrate on what they are saying and look interested.** You could even ask a few questions. But don't interrupt them too much.

And never try to turn the conversation around to you. They will like you better if you just let them talk.

○ **Be enthusiastic about the project.**

The director will want to work with people who are **enthusiastic about their project**. You don't have to compromise your true feelings, but if you want the job there will always be something about it that you find exciting.

○ **Ask them things about the project.**

If there is anything you don't understand about the project, or you want more information, just ask them.

○ **If necessary, take control of the meeting.**

Sometimes the meeting can be awkward and uncomfortable. If this is the case, you can **lead the conversation yourself.** Ask them questions and tell them things about yourself.

If you have had a **role in any plays or films** that are relevant to the project, it would be quite appropriate to mention them.

But if you find yourself talking too much, make sure you **leave little gaps so they can speak** if they want to. Don't just rabbit on without letting them get a word in edgeways.

A few things to avoid talking about

○ **Never pretend to know something you don't.**

It never works. They may ask, 'Have you seen (blah-di-blah)?' or 'Do you know (Thingummy Whatsit)?', and you may not have a clue what they're talking about. So just say 'no' and ask them to tell you more.

You are allowed to 'not know' things.

○ **Don't plead lack of time as an excuse for poor preparation.**

It will seem as if you're not interested in the project and your excuses will only make matters worse.

It's too late now anyway.

You should have prepared properly in the first place.

○ **Don't ever criticise other directors you have worked with.**

You may have worked with a director who is known to be mean, difficult or even useless, but if you are asked about them, be careful how you answer.

You don't want to come across as the sort of person who criticises directors behind their backs.

Not to another director.

They'll think you might be critical of them one day.

○ **Don't criticise the script.**

You may think it's awful and the director may even comment on how bad it is, but keep positive. Find the good points.

The director won't want actors grumbling about the script when everyone's working on it.

It creates a bad atmosphere.

Directors like to be surrounded by positive people.

The farewell

○ When the meeting appears to be over, keep relaxed, **but don't be the person to end it**.

○ Maybe the director or the casting director has more to say and it's just a brief pause while they give themselves time to think. If you try to finish the meeting during a brief pause in the conversation **it could look like you are in a hurry for it to be over**.

○ When the director or the casting director actually ends the meeting, **keep your exit short, sweet and polite**.

○ Don't try to prolong the meeting. They've seen enough to make a decision and **they want to get on with their work**.

○ When you finish, say something like 'It was good to meet you.'

It's important to maintain equal status right to the end.

A few things to avoid as you finish

○ **Don't say 'Thank you for seeing me.'**

It lowers your status. Anyway, they should be *thanking you* for *seeing them.*

○ **Don't say 'Good luck with the project.'**

It lowers *their* status. If the project needs 'luck' to succeed it sounds like you don't think it's very good.

○ **Don't try a last-minute plea for work.**

Avoid saying things like, 'I really want to be in this project,' or 'I'd love to work with you,' etc. It may be true but it makes you sound desperate.

The meeting is over.

Just finish calmly.

DIFFERENT TYPES OF MEETINGS

No two meetings are the same. The kind of jobs on offer are different. And the people you meet are different. But here are some examples that may help you be prepared.

But please remember *these are generalisations.*

The following information may not always be true.

_ But it's definitely worth considering. _

A live theatre audition

Generally speaking, theatre directors have a good understanding of how **actors think and work**. Especially if they have been actors themselves. This is handy because they understand that actors can **transform themselves and become someone else**.

So they don't expect you to be exactly like the character.

What to wear

Theatre directors may want to **work on a scene** with you to see how you **respond to direction**. You may be asked to move about the room, crawl across the floor, or jump up and down. Who knows?

So wear clothes that don't inhibit your movements.

- Wear something **loose or stretchy.**
- Wear **soft shoes** that won't slip on the floor if you're asked to run about.
- Don't wear anything that could expose parts of you **that you want to keep private when you move about.**
- Don't have a **complicated hairstyle** that may fall apart if you move your head too much.

But at the same time,

Make sure you don't look too scruffy!

It would be quite acceptable to change into **soft shoes** during an audition, or **remove a jacket,** but any other change of clothing could hold things up too much.

How to behave

Theatre directors understand an actor's **creative process** so when they ask you to do something, allow yourself to **behave the way you would in rehearsals.**

- **Ask questions** if anything needs clarification.
- **Take your time** to think about what you are being asked to do.
- And only start **when you are ready.**

The director may have ideas about the character or the play that are **different from yours.**

So have a brief discussion about these differences.

Explain your **point of view** and try to understand **the director's point of view.**

See if you can combine these two ways of thinking so **both of you are satisfied.**

But never block the direction.

Keep positive.

And make a full commitment when you are asked to do something.

A television audition

Television directors often come from more **technical backgrounds**. They may have been *camera operators*, *sound engineers* or *lighting designers*, and they often have **less understanding** of how actors transform into other characters.

So you need to give their imagination a helping hand.

What to wear

I would suggest you **'dress towards'** the character. Wear your **own clothes**, but choose an outfit will help them **imagine you** as the character you are auditioning for.

For example:

○ If you are auditioning for a character who is a doctor or a lawyer, **wear something smart**.

○ If you are auditioning for a character who is basically at home with their family, **wear something casual**.

○ If you are auditioning for a character who is out clubbing, **wear something that makes you look exciting and attractive**.

But never feel as if you are wearing a costume.

Wear your own clothes.

And choose an outfit that is a little like the character you are auditioning for.

How to behave

It would be very useful to watch something the director has directed in the past so you have an **opinion of their work**.

Their recent TV productions may still be online.

○ **Make mental notes** so you will be able to talk about the actors.

○ Pick out **particular scenes** that impressed you.

○ Check out any unusual **technical stuff**.

○ Analyse any exciting or complicated **action sequences**.

It would be quite appropriate to say you've **seen something** the director has worked on in the past.

Most people love to talk about the things they've done.

So mention the things you liked.

Be positive, be honest, but don't be ridiculously overenthusiastic.

Television Directors sometimes leave it up to **the casting director** to conduct the interview. But make sure you talk to **both of them** when you answer.

○ Avoid talking too much about **your own creative process** unless they appear to be interested.

○ Mention **positive things** about other people you have worked with.

○ Be **enthusiastic** about the project.

Television is often filmed on a very tight schedule, so when you are asked to read from the script, **don't try to discuss anything**, just get on with it.

○ Create a **clearly defined character**.

○ Make **positive choices** about the way you read the lines.

○ Imagine your face is **in close-up**.

○ Take your time to **react truthfully** to the lines the other person is reading. It's just as important as saying your own lines truthfully.

○ Create **interesting pauses**, but fill them with your thoughts.

A film audition

Big budget, small budget, it's all the same.

People who make movies are obsessed with the art.

They need to be, because it's all about **money**.

And money is extremely hard to find.

So when you are meeting a film director you need to realise that casting the actors comes towards **the end of a very lengthy process**.

Budget meetings.   Script meetings.   Location scouting.

Set-design meetings   Costume meetings.

And practically everything else.

Apart from actually filming the thing.

So meeting actors is where the fun starts.

At last, the film director is getting close to doing the thing **they like doing best.**

Making movies.

What to wear

The finances for making a film are often driven by the **box-office appeal of the actors**.

So directors cast as many well-known actors in their films as possible.

And well-known actors are often cast as characters who are **quite different** from themselves.

But unless you are **well-known**, most Film Directors like to cast actors who **closely resemble the characters** that they will be playing.

It's not that they lack imagination.

But there are **so many actors** to choose from and **'time is money'**, so it's better to cast an actor who will be able to play a character without any fuss.

This, of course, is called *typecasting*.

The casting director will probably have invited you to the casting session for several reasons:

a) You are **available for work** on the scheduled dates.

b) You are a **talented actor**.

c) Your agent will **accept the fee** being offered.

d) Your personality and appearance are both **very like the character**.

So when you are given the **character breakdown** or a **copy of the script** to read, all you have to do for the interview is **dress the way that you would dress** if you were doing **what the character does** in the film.

How to behave

As I said, casting is usually an enjoyable experience for the director.

Particularly if they have a good casting director.

○ So allow yourself to **join in the fun**.

○ Get involved in **the excitement**.

○ **And always be supportive**.

If you are asked to read a scene, try to do it exactly as you would if you were already in the film.

○ Get **inside the head** of the character you are playing.

○ Read the script like **your life depended on it**.

○ **Make major artistic decisions** and **play them to the hilt**.

○ **Have total commitment to your acting talent.**

If you do this, the director and the casting director will be **excited by your work**.

And they will want to put you in the film.

If they don't think you are suitable for this character,

they may ask you to read a different character.

And if there aren't **any suitable characters** for you in this film,

they'll remember you when they are making their next film.

And whether you get the part or not, they **will be excited about the way you behaved**.

And the casting director will remember you for future casting sessions.

And eventually the right part will come along.

And that's how it all works.

Commercial casting sessions

Okay, you didn't become an actor so you could make commercials, but they are **useful money-makers**, and that's better than working as a waitress or a barman.

So go for it!

But remember, generally speaking, the people who direct commercials have **no knowledge about acting at all**.

They will have a strong opinion about the role being cast and they want to see someone who is **exactly how they imagine the character to be**.

And the casting director will have invited you to the casting session because they think you are **exactly how the director imagines the character to be.**

What to wear

Simple answer:

Dress as the character.

How to behave

Your Agent will probably have told you exactly what they're looking for.

So listen to your agent.

And then behave the way the character would behave.

This won't be as difficult as it sounds because the casting director will have developed a **very clear idea of what you are actually like.** And you will be going up for parts that are **pretty much how you actually are.**

Easy-peasy!

Finally, a few words of advice about commercial casting sessions:

Smile and be friendly.

Listen carefully to any instructions.

Do exactly what they ask you to do.

And never make jokes about the product.

13. AUDITIONS AND READINGS

DIRECTORS

Having auditions and meetings is part of the actor's job.

But it can be **stressful**.

You have to be **at your best**.

You **don't get paid**.

It can be **time-consuming**.

And it's not always successful.

But actors spend their time wanting **more and more meetings** because that's the way **they get jobs**.

And they need jobs so they can practise their art.

But holding meetings and auditions can also be **quite hard for directors**.

They need to choose the right actors.

So *they* can practise *their* art.

So directors need to find out **a lot of things about you**.

○ What is your **background**?
○ Would the two of you **get on**?
○ What sort of **temperament** do you have?
○ Are you **confident** in yourself?
○ What kind of **roles** have you played?
○ Which **companies** have you worked for?
○ What **area of work** do you like doing?

This is reasonably straightforward. Directors will get **most of the information from an interview and your CV**.

But directors also have to find out a lot of other things:

○ Are you **suitable for the part**?
○ Are you **confident in your acting**?
○ Can you **take direction**?
○ Are you **creative**?
○ Will the two of you be able to **work together**?
○ Will you be **exciting** to work with?
○ **And are you the sort of actor that the director likes?**

And this is **a lot harder**.

So to find these things out, directors need to hold **some sort of audition**.

And they have a number of different ways of doing this.

AUDITIONS

Two prepared speeches

This is the sort of audition that you had to do **to get into drama school**.

And it's highly unlikely that you will ever have to do an audition like this professionally.

But it's possible.

So be prepared.

○ Find **two contrasting speeches** that are suitable for your **talent** and **personality**.
○ **Prepare them.**
○ **Keep them rehearsed** just in case.

(*Note: All the information you need about this is in Chapter Two.*)

READINGS

Reading for a part

This method of finding the right actor for a part is much more common.

○ Usually you will be sent **the script** a few days before the audition and asked to prepare a particular scene.

- ○ Sometimes you are **just sent a scene** (known as 'sides') because the project is a bit hush-hush.

  (*Note: If you are dyslexic it is perfectly acceptable to ask your agent or the casting director if you can see the script (or the scene) a few days before the meeting so you have time to prepare. This would also be acceptable for actors who are not dyslexic.*)

Preparation

- ○ If you've been sent the whole script, **read it carefully**.
- ○ **Then read it a second time**, making notes about your character.
- ○ If it's an adaptation of a novel, **read the novel** to learn as much about your character as you can.
- ○ **Learn the scene and practise it.**
- ○ If possible, get another actor to **read the scene with you**.
- ○ **Try doing it different ways.** You never know what they might ask you to do and it's good to **be prepared for any eventualities**.
- ○ If it's a scene with physical action, stand up and **practise it as if you were doing it for real**.

The meeting

Keep calm during the initial chat.

Don't think about the scene yet.

And don't fiddle with the script!

Taking control

When you are asked to **read the scene**, this is the moment when you should **take control of the audition**. They want to see you acting, and **acting is your area of expertise**.

So you are now in charge.

Don't start until you are ready.

- ○ If there is anything about the script, the scene or the character that you are unsure about, **ask them for more information**.
- ○ Tell them you have learned the scene, but **hold the script in your hand just in case**.

○ If the scene has physical action, say that you'd like to **get up and move around**.

Everyone wants actors who take responsibility for their work.

Show them that you are in control.

But don't waste too much time.

Working with the person reading with you

Sometimes the person reading the scene with you is **not particularly good at acting**.

But don't let that put you off.

Or affect the way you want to play the scene.

○ If the scene requires it, look the other person in the eyes and **speak the lines directly to them**. Even if they're not looking back at you.

○ If you are not 'getting anything back' from the other person, **behave as if you are**.

○ Make sure you are **listening and responding** to the other character in the scene.

○ If you are reading an intimate scene for television or film, play the scene as if it was **a close-up on you**.

○ If the reading is for a theatre project, **use whatever space there is available to move around**.

Responding to direction

Sometimes you will be asked to play the scene differently.

○ Be enthusiastic about the way you are being directed **even if you don't quite agree with it**.

○ Make sure you **fully understand** what you are being asked to do.

See if you can make adjustments **without compromising your own beliefs**.

○ Be **totally committed** to this new way of playing the scene.

Sometimes you will be asked to play **the character** differently.

○ **Be bold with any new ideas.** Run with them and enjoy them.

○ If you are asked to use a different accent, take a moment to try it out and then **just go for it**, even if you don't get it right.

○ Don't let any mistakes throw you. **Just stop and ask if you can start again.**

If you are struggling with a different way of doing the scene or playing the character, **don't let that make you insecure.**

You know you have the talent.

Sometimes new ideas need a bit of work to get them right.

These are *your skills* that are being auditioned.

○ **Keep positive.**
○ **Keep fully committed to your acting.**
○ **Surprise yourself with your talent.**

Take yourself seriously as an actor.

And they will take you seriously as well.

Cold readings

Sometimes you may be asked to read a **scene** or a **character** from a **script you have never seen before**. This is known as a **cold reading**.

Hopefully the director or the casting director will **give you information** about the scene and the character. Don't forget, **they** *want* **you to be perfect for the part** so they will be keen to help you.

○ Ask if you can have **a minute or two** to look at it before you start.
○ Make sure you have been given enough information about **the scene and the character**.

Preparation

○ **Practise reading unfamiliar texts** at home on a regular basis. Open any book at random and read out loud whatever you see on the page.
○ **Read 'ahead of yourself'.** As you finish reading a phrase, see if you can make sense of the next phrase before you actually say it. Then get used to making instant decisions about **variety of tone, mood and pace**.
○ **Don't read too fast.**
○ Imagine you are reading to someone else and **make sure the imaginary person understands what you are saying**.

○ **Get together with other actors** as often as you can and read scripts or plays together **that you've never seen before**. Not only will this be fun but it will expand your knowledge of other texts.

If you are asked to go to a meeting but **haven't been sent a script**:

Ask your agent or the casting director if a script will be available for you to look at if you arrive half an hour early for the meeting.

If they say 'I don't know', arrive half an hour early just in case.

And then ask again if there is a script you can look at.

IMPROVISATION IN AUDITIONS

Sometimes you will be asked to **improvise something** in an audition. This can be quite daunting because a large part of an actor's skill is how to **analyse a written text and make it truthful**.

When you are improvising, this skill isn't needed.

But all the other acting skills are.

○ The ability to **imagine you are someone else**.
○ The ability to view the world **from someone else's viewpoint**.
○ The ability to believe that you are in **a different location**.
○ The ability to have **a complex relationship with someone you hardly know**.

So my advice is to **concentrate on these acting skills**.

Because you *know* you are good at them.

○ Become **the character**.
○ Imagine you are in **the given situation**.
○ Imagine the people improvising with you are **the characters they are supposed to be**.
○ **Believe in the power of your imagination.**
○ Say the words that come into **your character's mind**.
○ **Be truthful** when you say them.

And above all...

Don't try to be entertaining or funny.

> **Just be real.**

SELF-TAPES

For **self-tapes**, which you film at home and send off, a small financial outlay will **save you money** in the long run.

Here's what you need:

- **A smartphone with a decent camera** – you can buy a small video camera, but nowadays everything can easily be done on your smartphone.

  (*Note: It's possible to do self-tapes on a computer or a laptop, but I recommend a smartphone because it's easier to position it so you are properly in the frame and well lit.*)

- A smartphone **tripod** – to keep the camera steady.

- **A light of some sort with its own tripod** – you need to be clearly lit without sharp or distracting shadows, so it is best to use a **light diffuser box**. If you can afford it, buy a SAD (seasonal affective disorder) lightbox because **it recreates natural light**.

- **A blank background** – don't let what's in the background be a **distraction** from your performance. If you can't film yourself in front of a blank wall, you can buy a **projection screen**, a **photographer's backdrop** or even **hang up a sheet** – nicely ironed, of course.

- A simple **editing app** – like iMovie or PowerDirector.

- An app for **sending videos** over the internet (like Vimeo or WeTransfer).

Full-body slate

A *full-body slate* is when they ask you to state your **name**, **height** and **agent** in a **full-length shot** at the start of a *self-tape*. You can record it separately from the acting scene and edit them together later.

As part of the slate, they sometimes ask for other pieces of information, such as:

- Your **location**, so they know which part of the world you are in.

○ To see you in **profile** – both sides.

○ To hold up your hands – front and back – so they can see them clearly.

Sometimes you may be asked to **tell them something about yourself and what you've been up to lately.** This is really just so that they can hear you speak, and get a sense of the 'real' you, when you're not playing the character.

○ Keep it **brief, chatty and friendly.**

○ Don't talk about **holidays, pets, hobbies, etc.,** unless specifically asked to.

○ Talk about the parts you've enjoyed playing recently.

Keep it short, sweet and an expression of your personality.

Script reading

Reading a self-taped scene will be like any other scene reading except you'll need to get **someone to help you** by reading in the other lines of dialogue.

They will be **behind the camera** and nearer to it, so ask them to **speak quite quietly**, otherwise they will be louder than you.

It doesn't really matter if the other person isn't very good at reading, as long as they don't **put you off.**

Anyway, you don't want them to be too good.

They may be more interesting than you!

Practise

○ Create a **character.**

○ **Learn the words** – if they've given you enough time.

○ **Practise the scene with someone** reading in the other lines.

Recording

○ The whole scene should be recorded in landscape orientation, and in a **mid-shot**, unless they say otherwise – top of the head to three-quarters of the way down your chest.

○ The person reading the other lines should stand **just behind the camera or smartphone and a little to one side,** so you can play the scene directly to them.

○ **Record the scene.**

○ Review it and **re-record it** if you're not satisfied.

○ **Edit in the full-body slate** if you were asked for one – this would usually be put in before the scene reading. But if you are playing a character with a different accent, you could consider putting the full-body slate after the scene. **If they hear your natural accent first**, they sometimes think that any other accent you use sounds phoney!

Even if it doesn't!

○ Send a copy of the self-tape to your **agent** – if there's time – so they can give you feedback and comments.

If all is well, it's ready to go.

Deadline

You will be given a deadline. If the tape is for a US casting, don't forget:

West Coast USA is usually 8 hours behind the UK.

(*Note: USA's Daylight Saving Time and British Summer Time may not change on the same date, so always check this out.*)

If they want to **receive a self-tape by 10.00 a.m. PST** (Pacific Standard Time) that means you don't need to send it to them till about **4.00 p.m. GMT** – a couple of hours early to be on the safe side.

However, it's probably best to send any self-tape **as soon as you can.** They will start reviewing them straight away, so there is no harm in **getting in early**.

ONLINE AUDITIONS

If you are doing a live audition online, instead of taping your scene and sending it off, you will have been told that the audition will be **at a particular time**.

So you need to be totally ready when the call comes in.

(*Note: Online auditions can also sometimes be with someone **in the USA**. Because of the time difference it will usually take place **in the*** *evening* if you're in the UK. Make sure you understand **the exact UK time that the audition will take place**.)

○ Get dressed in the **appropriate clothing**.

○ Put on any **make-up** that you need – everyone could use **a bit of foundation** to stop their faces looking too shiny, blotchy or red.

○ **It's probably best to do online auditions on a laptop or a computer so you can see the people you are talking to clearly.**

○ The **camera** in your laptop or computer should be **at eye-level**.

○ It's best to have **a completely blank wall** behind you.

○ Make sure you are **properly lit**, using your **diffuser light** if possible.

○ **Frame yourself** so they can see your **head and shoulders**.

○ Take a **practice video** of yourself.

○ Check the video and **reposition yourself** or the **diffuser light** if necessary.

○ Make any suitable adjustments to your **hair** and **make-up**.

○ Sit ready **five minutes before the appointed time** and wait for the online call.

○ **Answer the call** when it comes.

○ **Sit back down and follow their instructions.**

You will usually be given two or three days' notice to look at the scene, **so learn it**!

BUT... You can also **hang the script behind the camera** so it's in your eyeline. Then you will be able to **glance at it if you need to** and they won't even notice.

It will look like your character is thinking about things.

Practise

The main difficulty with an online audition is the delay.

You finish saying a line and the other person doesn't appear to answer for a second or two.

It's hard to handle.

So my advice is to practise reading with someone else and ask them to **delay their line** each time it's their cue.

That may help you get used to it.

○ Stay focused and **'in the scene'** during the delay.

○ **Have faith** that the other person **will actually say the next line** – when you are in a high-pressure situation, a **short pause** can feel like a **lifetime**.

CHEMISTRY READINGS

This is when two actors are going to play characters with **a strong relationship**.

○ A husband and wife.

○ Lovers.

○ Siblings.

○ War buddies.

○ Two private detectives working on the same case.

Anything that requires the actors to establish some sort of **'chemistry'** between them.

○ This could be romantic.

○ Sparky.

○ Funny.

○ Adventurous.

○ Confrontational, etc.

Creating a partnership

○ Sometimes a number of actors are auditioned for **one of the characters** and then another bunch of actors are auditioned for **the other character**.

○ Then **several possible 'pairings'** are decided by the director or casting director.

○ Each pair of actors are then **auditioned together** to see which pair has the right 'chemistry'.

Adding a partner

Sometimes a close partnership is needed between a **leading character** and a character who **only has a few scenes**.

○ **A well-known actor** has **already been cast** in the leading part.

- Other actors are then auditioned to read with the well-known actor to see who **creates the right 'chemistry'**.
- The well-known actor would then probably **have a say in the casting** of the other character.

Meeting the well-known actor

You and the actor need to develop a **mutual respect** for each other.

- Be **friendly**. But not over-friendly.
- Be **interested** in what the other actor has to say.
- State your own opinions **truthfully**.
- Look the other actor **in the eyes** when either of you are speaking.
- Treat the other actor like a **friend** and an **equal**, even if they are more experienced than you and have a much bigger part.

Reading a scene

- When you are talking about the scene, try to develop **a relationship with the leading actor**.
- When you are reading a scene, try to develop a relationship **between the two characters**.
- **Enjoy being with the well-known actor** and they will probably enjoy being with you.

Finally

If there is no 'chemistry' between you, there is nothing you can do about it.

It's nobody's fault.

RECALLS

It's great to get a recall, but when you are on your **seventh recall** for the same part, it can be a bit of a nightmare.

- **First recall** – They **like you** and want to see more.
  Relax! Just keep doing **what you did last time**.
- **Second recall** – They still **like you**, but they like a couple of other actors as well.

Relax! Just keep doing **what you did last time.**

○ **Third recall** – The director **still likes you,** but maybe **the Producer needs to see you** before the deal is finalised.

Relax! Just keep doing **what you did last time.**

○ **Subsequent recalls** – Don't despair. **They still like you, but they can't make up their mind.**

There's nothing different you can do about it.

Relax!

Just keep doing what you've always done.

KEEP A RECORD OF ALL YOUR MEETINGS

It's surprising how easy it is to **forget the details of a meeting,** and there is **every chance** you will meet the director or the casting director again in the future.

So **buy a notebook** or **create a spreadsheet on your computer** to keep a record of all the meetings you have.

1. **The time and date** – so you know exactly when it was.

2. **The location** – so you know **exactly where** the meeting took place. Was it online or in an office, a studio, a theatre or a coffee bar?

3. **The director** – and what they were like.

4. **The casting director** – and what they were like.

5. **The project** – did it sound interesting?

6. **The role** – what kind of character were you being auditioned for?

7. **What you talked about** – this is important.

8. **How you felt during the meeting** – were you confident, happy, relaxed, etc.?

9. **How you think the meeting went** – be honest.

10. **Whether or not you got the job!** – maybe you turned it down.

These notes will help if you have a **second meeting** with the director or the casting director.

○ So you will be **better prepared**.
○ You will be **more relaxed**.
○ You will be able to **talk about the first meeting**.

And you won't be taken by surprise.

Without these notes you might recognise the director **but not remember where or when you met**.

○ Your mind could go **blank** – particularly in a **stressful situation** like an interview or audition.
○ And you will feel **useless**.

And there is no way you want to feel useless.

So before you go for a meeting or an audition:

○ **Read through your notes** to see if you've met the director or the casting director before.
○ If you have met them before, remind yourself **what they were like**.
○ Check out how you **felt about the meeting**.
○ Remember what **the project** was.

Then you'll be properly prepared.

And you'll feel more confident.

PERSONAL DEBRIEF

You are bound to analyse **each moment of a meeting** after it has finished, but to be quite honest,

There's no point.

It's impossible to guess what the director might have been thinking.

Each director is different.

Each and every meeting is different.

So as long as you were **well prepared** and you **presented yourself in a positive manner**,

There was nothing more you could have done.

Here's a major reality check:

There are a lot of talented actors available for each job.

Many who would be the right casting.

IF YOU DON'T GET THE JOB IT'S RARELY A REJECTION OF YOUR TALENT.

Remember that.

IT'S RARELY A REJECTION OF YOUR TALENT.

Write that on the wall.

CONCLUSION

When all's said and done, it's not just up to you to make the meeting go well.

It's up to both you and the director.

And if a director makes you feel uncomfortable,

Or appears to dislike you,

Then you probably wouldn't have enjoyed working with them anyway!

14. THE BIG WIDE WORLD – OR YOUR FIRST JOB AND BEYOND

GETTING WORK

There are four possible outcomes for you at the end of a drama training course.

1. **You have a job and an agent** – That's brilliant. You're up and running.

2. **You have a job but *no agent*** – Pretty good. You're a professional actor.

3. **You have an agent but *no job*** – Almost as good. Maybe there's a job round the corner.

4. **You have *no agent* and *no job*** – Difficult. What should you do next?

Oh, and there's a fifth possible outcome of course.

5. **You've given up the idea of an acting career** – Oh well. That's life. Good luck with whatever you do next.

But it doesn't matter which of the first four outcomes is your situation.

You are still an actor.

But there will often be times when you feel like you'll never work again.

So remember this:

Everything could change tomorrow

Or next week

Or at any time in the future.

You have a job and an agent

This feels like the perfect outcome, and in lots of ways it is. **But you've still got to keep focused on the rest of your career.**

You have an agent, so you feel like there's someone looking after you, but that's not entirely true.

They've got loads of clients to think about.

And you can't always rely on your agent to get you interviews.

So you must keep working on your career yourself:

○ Meet up socially with any **industry professionals** that you know.

○ If you're in a play, invite **casting directors** and **directors** to see your performance.

○ If you're working on a film, use the **internet** to let people know about it.

○ Always keep your **online information** up to date.

○ Make regular use of your **social media** accounts to keep reminding people that you exist.

○ **And don't forget to meet up with other actors.**

You have a job but no agent

Great. You're working. This is the perfect time to promote yourself. So follow all the advice above.

But also contact agents right now.

Especially agents you've met before.

○ If you're in a play, **invite them to see it**.

And meet them socially afterwards.

○ If you're in a film, **let them know about it**.

And invite the agent you want to represent you to the film premiere.

You have an agent but no job

Agents are all different, but they have one thing in common:

They want to get work for their clients.

And they will be trying to find suitable roles for you.

All the time.

But you must work with them:

○ **Keep yourself looking good** in case your agent has an audition for you tomorrow.

It won't help you get the job if you are tired, hungover or need a haircut.

○ **Let your agent know about any casting sessions** that you think would be right for you.

Agents are usually pretty well-informed about casting sessions, but they may easily have **overlooked a job** that another actor has told you about.

○ Always **accept an audition** that your agent puts you up for. **And thank them.**

They've **done their work** so the least you can do is **to be properly prepared**.

Always turn up early for live casting sessions.

Always be set up and ready for an online session.

○ Let your agent know if you are **going to be away** for any length of time.

You may not have heard from your agent for a while, but they need to know where you are in case a **suitable role** is being cast.

○ If you have been **offered a job** and **don't want to do it**, discuss it properly with your agent.

○ If you get a job offer that **your agent doesn't know about**, always **tell them before you accept it.**

They may be in the process of getting you an interview for a **much better job**, which could clash with the one you've been offered.

○ Work with your agent to plan your career.

At this stage they know more about the business than you do. So **trust them** and **listen to their advice**.

You have no agent and no job

This is obviously the **worst position** to be in.

OR IS IT ??

If you have no agent and no job, you are going to be **much more motivated** to get yourself some work.

And self-motivation is a powerful thing.

But how are you going to go about it?

And what should you do?

Answer:

> **Do anything you can!**

But above all:

Don't lose faith.

Don't give up.

Keep positive.

And surround yourself with supportive people.

HOW TO FIND OUT ABOUT CASTINGS

Friends

A lot of your friends will probably be ex-students like you.

In other words, they'll be actors.

And they'll each have **information about casting sessions** through their agents or people they might be working with.

- ○ So meet up with **ex-students**.
- ○ Develop relationships with **friends who are actors**.
- ○ Chat with them about **what's going on**.
- ○ **And never feel that being unemployed means you're not talented.**

Mandy

Mandy is a **website** where **directors** and **casting directors** post information about the projects they are casting.

These postings include work in:

Theatre Films Television drama

Role-play work Corporate work Extra work

Children's theatre Advertising campaigns

And they need actors for all of these!

But they also post information about jobs for:

Singers Dancers Musicians

Voice-over artists Child actors

In fact, any kind of work that needs **performers**.

Directors and _casting directors_ post new jobs on Mandy every day.

Agents use Mandy.

You can use it too.

You can log in to mandy.com for **free** and it will give you information about **unpaid work** or jobs that are **expenses only**.

But if you are **serious about looking for work**, you can **pay a subscription** and take advantage of all Mandy's benefits.

Backstage

Backstage (backstage.com) also has information about **casting**. Both paid and unpaid work. It's based in the USA, but you can search for **job opportunities in London**.

Spotlight

You will be in Spotlight so you should make use of all the **graduate benefits** they have on offer.

○ Free admission to **talks from industry professionals** – They do talks on *voice-over* work, *acting for camera*, *commercials*, etc. All the information is on their website, **spotlight.com**.

○ Free **career advice** – You can get career advice from someone at Spotlight by arranging to talk to them on the phone, or online.

○ Details of **jobs** – You can log on to the website to get information about **jobs that are casting** and then, if you are not represented by an agent, you can **submit yourself for work**.

Actors Pro Expo

This organisation (actorsproexpo.com) is full of extremely useful information for actors:

○ They run **seminars** and **trade shows** for actors.

○ They have links to **workshops** and **acting classes**.

○ They run online **networking** sessions.

HOW TO KEEP INVOLVED

It's important to stay connected with the industry in **any way you can**, otherwise you will feel you're drifting away from it.

○ Go to **plays on press nights** and see if you can chat to any **directors**, **casting directors** and other **actors** that you may have met before.

○ Be on the lookout for **cheap West End theatre tickets** – At the time of writing, **TodayTix** is a great app for cheap ticket deals.

○ Watch **drama on TV** with other actors and talk about the performances.

○ Arrange to do **regular play-readings** with other actors.

HOW TO KEEP BEING CREATIVE

Drama is a collaborative art form so it's hard to do it on your own. But there are still ways to flex your creative muscles:

○ **Write scripts** for you and your actor friends, and get together to rehearse them.

○ Make your own **videos** and, if they're really good, upload them on YouTube or Vimeo.

○ Make sure your *showreel* is up to date.

HOW TO GET AN AGENT

You probably still feel that an agent will be able to help you with your career, so it's a good idea to keep trying to find one.

○ Contact agents by email on a **regular basis**.

○ Send them a link to your **profile** on **Spotlight**.

○ Send them a link to any **showreel** updates.

When you haven't got an agent and you're **not working**, this is a bit like throwing a handful of gravel high in the air and **hoping a stone will fall into a tin cup**.

But guess what?

It sometimes does.

And if you don't keep trying, it *never* will.

Actors' co-ops

An actors' co-op is formed when a group of actors get together to create **their own agency**.

It works like any other agency except it's **run by the actors**. They each spend a certain amount of time in the office **working as an agent**.

Positives

○ You are **involved in the industry** even when you're not working.

○ You can enjoy **promoting other people in the co-op**.

○ You are **well informed** about casting opportunities.

○ You can **put yourself up** for suitable roles through the agency.

Negatives

○ They are sometimes just as **difficult to join** as a regular agent.

○ Directors and casting directors find it difficult to make personal connections with a co-op because they **never know who they are going to be talking to.**

But it's worth considering.

Some actors just love it.

HOW TO EARN MONEY

In order to pay the bills, a lot of actors get work in **pubs** and **restaurants**, but that often means working **long hours** and **late nights.**

And the work can be pretty soul-destroying.

Especially when customers make jokes about 'resting' actors.

Some actors get work in **call centres.**

But that can also be a bit demoralising.

Especially when you are talking to negative people.

Who blame you for everything.

So it's probably best to get work with someone that **understands an actor's life.**

And will give you time off for auditions and meetings.

Flexible work

There is some great advice about flexible work on indeed.com.

Another actor-friendly company for finding work is *Chimera Recruitment* on the website chimerarecruitment.com.

It was founded by actors.

And offers flexible work in promotions and retail.

All sorts of other work is available online.

Just google 'jobs for actors' and you'll get a bunch of hits.

Actor's skills

It's best to look for work where you can use any particular skills you might have.

○ **Teaching**

You have been in acting classes for the last few years, so you will have a fair idea how to teach acting.

So look for jobs teaching drama to children.

(*Note: You will need a DBS check for any work that involves close contact with children. More information can be found online.*)

○ **Promotion**

As an actor you are experienced in speaking in front of a lot of people. You know how to be charming and you know how to improvise.

So promotion work is something you can do easily.

○ **Role-play**

Playing a role is a skill that all actors have, and the corporate world often uses actors in role-play situations to train their staff.

So check out role-play work.

○ **Children's entertainer**

Okay, so this might not be why you became an actor, but you certainly have the skill to do it. And it's great fun.

Find a job as a children's entertainer.

Or set up your own small business for local children's parties.

○ **Front-of-house**

A lot of actors get front-of-house work in West End theatres. It means you're **available for auditions** during the day. And front-of-house staff are often offered **free tickets** for shows in other theatres, although it can be a bit disheartening to watch other actors on the stage.

But at least it's part of the industry that you have joined.

And other front-of-house staff are probably actors too.

And they may know about casting sessions.

Other skills and qualifications

You can also use other **non-acting skills** or **qualifications** to make money.

You can **teach** anything that you're good at:

A musical instrument   Dancing   Singing

You can **help people** with their household chores:

Painting and decorating   Gardening   Carpentry   Cleaning

You can **look after people** and animals:

Care work   Childminding   Dog walking
(*Note: DBS may be needed*)

You can run sessions to help people **keep healthy**:

Yoga   Martial arts   Sports   Fitness

It's important to find a job that you **enjoy** while you search for proper **acting work**.

And helping other people is extremely rewarding.

AN ACTOR'S LIFE

We all hear stories about Hollywood actors earning **millions of dollars** per film, but every single one of them started out with nothing.

Struggling to get a job.

And **very few actors** earn all their money from acting.

Definitely not in the first few years.

And **no actors** are always in work.

In fact, unemployment is part of the actor's life.

'If you're an actor, even a successful one, you're still waiting for the phone to ring.' *Kevin Bacon*

But an actor's life can **never be boring** because it's totally **unpredictable**.

So celebrate that fact.

And never compare your career to anyone else's.

'Everybody hacks their own path through the jungle.'
Peter Ustinov

And when people **outside the profession** refer to actors as 'luvvies', just remember:

They know nothing about an actor's life.

They know nothing about the job.

And they've entirely missed the point.

Actors *aren't* 'luvvies':

They're artists.

They're adventurers.

They are 'the abstract and brief chronicles of the time'.
Shakespeare

And in the *Vagrancy Act of 1714* they are fabulously identified as:

'Rogues and vagabonds.'

The last bit of advice:

Acting is a dangerous job.

○ **Searching for work** is challenging.

○ **Rehearsing with people you've just met** is emotionally stressful.

○ **Revealing your inner emotional life** to relative strangers makes you vulnerable.

○ **Discovering the essence of a character** is sometimes mystifying.

○ **Performing in front of hundreds of strangers** is like walking into a pack of wild animals.

○ **Reading unfair, negative reviews** is totally demoralising.

○ **And being unemployed again** can send you plunging back into hopeless desperation and misery.

In fact, there are a **million things that can go wrong** at every stage of an actor's journey.

So actors sometimes combat this by being **superstitious**.

They trust their luck to the gods.

Over the years actors have had many different superstitions, but there is one that remains constant:

Actors think that wishing each other good luck

Is bad luck.

So they don't do it.

Instead they say 'Break a leg'.

So my final message to you all is this:

Trust your own judgement.

Live your life on the edge.

Rejoice in your artistic creativity.

AND BREAK A LEG, ALL YOU ROGUES AND VAGABONDS.